THE OIL BUSINESS AS I SAW IT

W. L. Connelly

THE OIL BUSINESS AS I SAW IT

Half a Century with Sinclair

NORMAN: UNIVERSITY OF OKLAHOMA PRESS

Library of Congress Catalog Card Number: 54–10213

Copyright 1954 by the University of Oklahoma Press
Publishing Division of the University
Composed and printed at Norman, Oklahoma, U.S.A.
by the University of Oklahoma Press
First edition

To the Memory of My Beloved Wife
Who, for More Than Fifty-five Years,
Put up with
the Trials and Tribulations of an Oilman

FOREWORD

THE LITERATURE of the country is becoming rich in the biographies of individuals who have contributed to the American advance in science, in industry, and in politics. However, there has been a notable dearth of what might be called biographies of business organizations. This book is not in any sense an attempt at one, but it gives an idea in typical American style of the stuff from which corporations are made.

This volume tells of men and their methods, of ventures and adventures, of the pioneering instincts which actuated those who lived and moved in a time that was ripe from their exploits. While the incidents recounted are unrelated, nevertheless when fitted together they cast a shadow which is recognizable as the early profile of the Sinclair Oil Corporation.

The author, William L. Connelly, long regarded as the dean of petroleum executives in the great Midcontinent area, has been persuaded to record these recollections. Perhaps without intent, he tells about the laying of foundations upon which are built many of our great business structures. Through the knowledge born of daily business contact for many years, he reveals the strength and driving force of Harry F. Sinclair, which ultimately resulted in the great company bearing his name. The biography of this company is still to come, but the present work of Mr. Connelly's is an absorbing forerunner which will be greeted with interest by oilmen everywhere. Much too rare in the petroleum industry are volumes like this one. Much too seldom have men of Mr. Connelly's vast experience and knowledge taken the pains to present the industry lore which is petroleum's.

P. C. LAUINGER

Tulsa, Oklahoma
May 24, 1954

SPUDDING IN

FOR MORE than sixty years my work has been oil. Thus it is that, on approaching the job of making a book, the term "spudding in" comes to mind, for in oil-field jargon that describes the initial step in drilling a cable-tool well.

It has been suggested to me many times that a narrative of my experiences in an industry which has revolutionized the world's way of life should be preserved in printed form. It was not without misgivings that I decided to undertake the task involved, for I have no false notions about my qualifications for it. I am an oilman, not a writer.

It is true, however, that my life has touched virtually every phase of the oil business. I have been a roustabout, pumper, foreman, district superintendent, landman, and division superintendent. I have been vice president, president, and chairman of the board of many companies, the highest of these official posts being vice president of the Sinclair Consolidated Oil Corporation. I was president of the Venezuela Petroleum Corporation. Recently I resigned as chairman of the board of the Sinclair Oil and Gas Company.

In the interests of my company I have visited Canada, Mexico, Venezuela, Colombia, Russia, Germany, France,

Italy, Switzerland, Panama, Costa Rica, Portugal, and Angola, West Africa. I have traveled horseback; in buckboards and automobiles; on freight trains, de luxe trains, and private cars; on slow and small steamers, luxurious liners, and airplanes; and once for a short distance in Russia, on a camel.

Owing to my long association with Harry F. Sinclair and the Sinclair companies, much of my story will naturally center around them. It will embrace other important companies. I have been associated with Harry Sinclair from 1906 to the present day.

What I personally have done or failed to do is not of consequence here, except as it throws sidelights on a stirring time in a marvelously interesting business. But I submit that many of the events described, the men who figured in them, and the spirit in which those men worked and played are of significance, for they had a part in the shaping of a nation.

So, with some qualms, I send this story on its way. If the indulgent reader gets as much pleasure out of reading it as I have had in putting it together, we both shall be happy. Especially do I hope that those of my friends who participated in incidents recounted will find enjoyment in reawakened memories. For they know, along with me, the adventure, the good luck and the bad, that have marked a fascinating field of work.

For their help in providing information and checking details in this account, I wish to express my deep appreciation to C. C. McDermond, E. L. Steiniger, C. F. McGoughran, Elbert Isom, Joseph von Beverin, F. H. Rhees, and W. F. McBreyer.

W. L. CONNELLY

Tulsa, Oklahoma
April 7, 1954

CONTENTS

ILLUSTRATIONS

THE OIL BUSINESS AS I SAW IT

1

THE OIL REGION BECKONS

MY FATHER, William Connelly, and his brother, Uncle John A. Connelly, were running a boiler shop at 27 Center Street, Cleveland, Ohio, at the time of my birth in that city on January 31, 1873 (a long time ago).

The young oil region of Pennsylvania had begun to stir wide interest, and it was recognized that a budding industry was offering a promising field for shops like the one Father and Uncle John operated in Cleveland. So plans for expansion were soon laid. Father opened a boiler shop and hardware store (that is what they called supply stores in those days) in Petrolia, and Uncle John set up a similar business in Bruin. These two Pennsylvania oil-boom towns were in Butler County.

The industrial events in which my family were involved during the first half-dozen years of my life made no profound impression upon me. Nor did the budding oil industry in which my people became quickly and inextricably interested. I was simply aware that they existed. But in the then roistering oil-boom town of Petrolia occured a misadventure which might easily have forestalled this book, besides reducing drastically the ultimate number of living Connellys. I was only six at the time.

At the rear of the shop operated by Father flowed Bear Creek. Ordinarily a well-behaved stream, it was given now and then to boisterous moods. At this point, a small island poked its head above the water. On the island stood a large but unimpressive wooden structure called the Coliseum. The building was devoted primarily to the seven-day walking matches popular in that period. Cash prizes and a championship belt went to winners. Passage to the island was by way of a crude bridge.

On July 21, 1879, while one of these walking matches was in progress, Father got word that a man who owed him money and who studiously avoided payment had been noticed entering the Coliseum. He decided forthwith to go over and see if he couldn't collect. My plea that I be allowed to go with him was granted. The creek was high, but there was no sign of danger. Reaching the Coliseum, we took seats while Father glanced about in a search for the slippery individual with whom he sought an interview.

Suddenly, before anybody could reach safety, a billowing mass of water inundated the island, swept the building from its foundations, and carried it downstream along with a crazy assortment of debris. Crushed barns, oil derricks, chicken coops, lumber, pigpens, and old-fashioned privies whirled about and bumped each other. Folk who a few minutes earlier had been occupied with nothing more exciting than a somewhat monotonous endurance test were now bobbing about in the swirling current, clutching at anything that offered hope of escape.

This startling conversion of an untroubled scene into one of terrifying confusion had been caused by one of the so-called flash floods which at times turned Bear Creek into a roily river. No flood like this one, however, had ever before been experienced. A torrential rainfall farther up the creek valley had rapidly swollen the little stream into a racing tide, which overran its banks and left ruin in its wake.

When the swiftly rising swell caught the Coliseum, my father grasped me, but he himself was struck by something in the wreckage and suffered a leg fracture, thus losing his grip on me. But he succeeded in reaching home safely. Meanwhile, a man named Blackburn drew me up on a log with him. Thus insecurely balanced, we sailed downstream. After a precarious voyage of several miles, Mr. Blackburn managed to get us ashore, but not on our side of Bear Creek.

It was late that night when I got home, a drenched, bedraggled figure. My parents were frantic, for they had received no word concerning my fate. My safe arrival caused an outburst of joy, but I was disconsolate. I had lost my hat.

The Coliseum never was rebuilt. Bear Creek later became a subdued little stream flowing meekly between banks about fifteen feet apart. The space once occupied by the island is now the site of a pretty school ground.

By this time, Father and Uncle John had sold their interest in the Cleveland boiler shop to my Uncle Dan Connelly. The shop subsequently fattened on the growing oil business and on the growth of the city itself, and ultimately became one of the largest enterprises of its kind in the United States. It remained in the ownership of Uncle Dan's family for more than sixty years, until 1937, when it was sold to the Babcock & Wilcox Company, and its last manager of the family name, W. C. Connelly, the eldest son of Uncle Dan, left it and subsequently became president of the Ohio Seamless Tube Company.

By 1880, Bradford became the oil region's red-hot town, and we moved there from Petrolia in 1882. Arriving at Bradford late in the afternoon, we took a hack (horse-drawn, of course) to the St. James Hotel, at the end of Main Street, five or six blocks from the depot. The streets were unpaved, and we became stuck in the mud several times on the short route to our destination.

After we had settled ourselves in the town, Father and Uncle Tom Connelly (it must be apparent by now that the Connellys were and are a numerous family) opened a boiler-repair shop there. In a short time they also began to develop some oil production on their own account. Father built a house at 95 Congress Street, where we lived for the several years that we remained in Bradford.

I attended St. Bernard School at first, and later the Public School on Congress Street. One winsome teacher in the latter, Miss Barr, captured my juvenile adoration. It was a hopelessly one-sided romance, for she had no suspicion of the heart-fluttering interest she had awakened. After the lapse of seventy years, she remains in my memory a fine lady. While living in Bradford, I made my only stage appearance in a school play at the Wagner Opera House. The play was *Snow White, the Fairy Queen, and the Seven Dwarfs*. Florence Haskell, now Mrs. Ed Bartlett of Tulsa, Oklahoma, was also in the cast.

I had an evening paper-route and sold the *Bradford Star*, which we boys called out as the "Even Ink Star."

Among the few people I know now living who attended school with me is Harold Cosgrove of Tulsa. A few former schoolmates may still be living in Bradford. Here in school I met Tom Donoghue, who was to become first vice president of the Texas Company. We were to be neighbors in Houston, Texas, and to have much business together there. John H. Markham, Jr., was a fellow student. John, who later made a profound impression upon the oil industry, and I were to be associated in many transactions in Tulsa. Bradford has furnished citizens for many towns in the oil states—Sistersville, West Virginia; Toledo and Lima, Ohio; Robinson, Illinois;

Tulsa, Oklahoma; Fort Worth and Houston, Texas, and many others.

For the generations as yet unborn during my Bradford years I should perhaps explain what the world looked like at the time. Society then was dependent upon the horse and buggy for local transportation, and roads of the period were rough, often muddy, and rutted. In dry weather they produced a considerable amount of dust. We had trains and the telegraph, but the telephone was so recent as to be a curiosity rather than a common means of communication.

To say that society was simple is to invite a complicated explanation. We were in those days still hewers of wood and drawers of water. For women who cooked over wood- or coal-burning stoves, life was anything but simple; and for boys who had to care for horses and see to a multitude of household chores, there was less time for mischief than may have become the case in a later day. We had no movies, no electric lights, much less any others like the modern-day triumphs of radio and television. If there had been a Hopalong Cassidy in my boyhood, none of us could have known about him except through the dime novels of Messrs. Beadle and Adams, common enough, it is true, but not always available to growing youngsters.

It is a little hard, even for me, to think of a time three-quarters of a century ago when the automobile was still a distant development. The question may logically be asked, therefore, "Why was Bradford so bustling a place?" The answer is the oil of Pennsylvania was used for kerosene lamps, for the lubrication of a growing American industry, for overseas trade, and even for medicinal purposes. The need for gasoline and for canned lubricants was not yet. But the aggregate consumption of oil was even then quite great. Bradford was the heart of oil production in that era.

Actually, we were then only a quarter of a century away

from the beginnings of domestic oil production, for the first of the Pennsylvania wells, the Drake, had been drilled in at Oil Creek in August, 1859. Many hundreds of miles away, in the Indian Territory, the Ross well was brought in the same year, but the area in which it was developed could have no bearing upon the oil industry for many years to come, nor upon my own career until even later.

Whale oil, for illumination, was far from obsolete in the world of my boyhood. The facilities for distributing refined petroleum were still primitive. Except for the gathering of oil in limited field areas, pipe lines were a development of the future. Artificial gas was almost everywhere current, and it supplied most of the illuminating, and a small part of the heating, requirements of large cities.

It was a time, also, of great mobility on the part of individuals and of families. We Irish, once transplated to the New World, knew no hindrances to movement. Late in my grade-school career, we moved from Bradford back to Cleveland, where we lived a short time. There I attended St. Patrick's School and later St. Ignatius' Preparatory School, now John Carroll University. The Lima oil fields were just getting into full swing when we moved, once more, to Toledo, Ohio. Father had a boiler shop there. I was now old enough to be employed as one of the office force and to make trips to towns in the oil fields. During these trips I met men who were to become lifelong friends and with whom I was to have substantial business dealings. Among them were D. J. O'Day, Mart Moran, Jim McMahon, Joe Dutton, Joe Dowling, and many more whose names are now part of the essential history of the American petroleum industry.

The Toledo boiler shop was destroyed by fire, and, with but little insurance to meet this loss, my father was out of business. This disaster prompted me to start a small boiler repair shop at Woodville, Ohio, and later one at Prairie Depot, Ohio. At Woodville I met A. H. (Herb) Black, who had a small tank shop not far from my boiler shop. Here began a friendship which has lasted through the years. Herb subsequently became a successful businessman and one of the most industrious I ever knew. He went on to organize the Black, Sivalls and Bryson Tank Company, which, after many years of operation, he sold for several million dollars. At Prairie Depot I became acquainted with Jim O'Neill, who in later years was to head the Prairie Oil and Gas Company and become an officer of the Standard Oil Company of New Jersey. In these connections I was to have many dealings with him, and our acquaintance ripened into warm friendship.

During the period I ran the little boiler shop at Prairie Depot I went out with different crews to make repairs on drilling or lease boilers. While I was repairing a boiler on a lease for Nolan and Griffin, Henry Harmon, a farmer, asked me if I knew anybody who would drill a well on his farm. I told him I would find someone. I went to Toledo, where I talked with Charley Johnson and Herman Phillips. We agreed that each of us should take a one-third interest in the drilling of the well, and we put up a deposit of three hundred dollars, which was to be forfeited in case we did not start the well in the time specified. I didn't have one hundred dollars. I went to Spencer D. Carr, the president of the Ketcham National Bank in Toledo, and told him my situation. He lent me the hundred on an unsecured note. To this day I wonder why he let me have the money. But that money started me in the oil business.

It must be kept in mind at this point that drilling costs in that period were insignificant in comparison with those which prevail today. A complete outfit of cable tools could be purchased for not more than three thousand dollars. A rotary rig today, to drill to a depth of fifteen thousand feet, costs from five hundred thousand to six hundred thousand dollars, depending upon the amount of stand-by equipment.

Johnson and Phillips were my first partners in the producing business. We three acquired forty acres (Harmon and Whitman Farm) near Plain Church, about six miles west of Prairie Depot, in Wood County, Ohio. Our first well came in for about one hundred barrels daily, and for the first oil we sold we received $1.27 a barrel (North Lima prices). We drilled several additional wells and then sold the property.[1]

Then in 1896, at the age of 23, I joined James Donnelly, J. E. Quinn, Michael Donnelly, and A. K. Detweiler in organizing the Donnelly Oil Company. James Donnelly and Quinn were personal friends of mine. Our first wells were drilled in the East Toledo field and at Curtis, Ohio. We also drilled a number in Wood County.

When I proposed to, and was accepted in marriage by, Miss Elizabeth Conlisk a couple of years later, the pattern of my roving life in the oil business was already pretty well defined, and she must have known it. Despite the prospect that I should be often absent from home, she joined me at the altar of St. Patrick's Church in Toledo, before the Reverend Edward Hannin, on October 4, 1898. However many the miles of distance that may have separated us at times, we really were never apart in all those years.

---

[1] A copy of the lease agreement for this, my first oil venture, appears in the Appendix to the present volume.

2

FOLLOWING THE TREND WESTWARD

I HAD NOT been part of the oil business long when some of its folklore became standard equipment with me, at least for the time being. "Doodlebug" and "oil-smeller" are terms applied to the curious array of oil-finding devices which once had a large and enthusiastic following. The geologist and geophysicist, plodding their precise and painstaking ways in the middle of the twentieth century, are able to locate underground structures favorable to the accumulation of oil, but they leave it to the drill to determine whether oil is actually present.

In contrast with the conservative attitude maintained by the scientific explorer, the man with an oil-finder was usually very positive concerning his ability to pick the exact spot where oil was to be found. And sometimes, the laws of chance being what they are, he did it, too.

Pithole, in Venango County, Pennsylvania, considered by some the most spectacular boom town in the annals of petroleum, owed its brief, robust career to a well drilled before my time, in January, 1876, four miles from the nearest previous production on a site selected by Thomas H. Browne with the guidance of a hazel twig. The well came in flowing

11

650 barrels daily, with oil selling at eight dollars a barrel. Ninety days later a city with an estimated population of sixteen thousand had sprouted around the spot. But production suddenly fizzled and the miracle city vanished as swiftly as it had risen.

Among queer superstitions which were slow dying was one that if a dry stake was used in marking the location for a well the well would be a failure. A green stake, cut from a living tree, was insisted upon. Dry stake, dry hole; green stake, wet hole, was the formula. Preparations for drilling a well in a western field were under way one day when a workman started to drive a location stake, using a stick from a seasoned board. Observing this blunder, the superintendent barked, "What the hell are you doing there? Want this to be a dry hole? Pull that stake out and get a green one!"

Before geology began to play an important part in the finding of oil we looked for scrub oaks and creeks as indications of oil deposits. As a matter of fact, it is pretty difficult to explain the term "wildcatter" (one who discovers oil where others did not know, or would not believe, that it could exist) except in terms of this kind of judgment. Those who succeeded at it in the early days of the oil business used the knowledge and the intuition (mostly intuition) available at the time. While I was not early in my career, nor subsequently, a wildcatter, I think I know what a man has to substitute for geological and geophysical knowledge when neither has yet been developed for oil exploration purposes.

In August, 1897, I saw for the first time a really big well drilled in. It was known as the "Klondyke." An "oil-smeller," as we called "doodlebugs" in those days, had located a well on a small tract of land (Miller Farm) east of Ironville, Ohio. Ironville was six or seven miles east of Toledo. Farther east than where this well was located were some small pools.

The doodlebugger was from Napoleon, Ohio, and he had

induced some friends of his in that town to put up the money to drill the well. The contract to drill (with cable tools, of course) was given to Stickle and Byers. Billy Stickle was the father of Frank Stickle, now of Tulsa. Elwood Byers later became an associate of mine in the Byers Drilling Company in Oklahoma. The two men had taken a small interest in the well.

The men who were putting up the money for the drilling were novices in the business and made no attempt to secure leases on any tracts save the one that they were to drill on. As a result, other oil men leased the acreage around the Miller Farm. Most of the tracts were small, from town lots to small farms, and none was larger than forty acres.

I had taken a lease on one of these tracts and was much interested in the Miller well for that reason and because the site had been determined by an oil-smeller. Later I sold an interest in the lease.

On the day that the sand (the Trenton Rock) was reached, I was at the well. The sand was penetrated for about fifty feet, the customary depth in those days, and was absolutely dry. Not even a rainbow of oil could be detected on the water. Gloom prevailed. The locater had predicted at least a 1,000-barrel well.

It was decided to give the well a shot of nitroglycerin. As I remember, a fair-sized shot was used, maybe 80 or 100 quarts. The result was amazing to those of us who watched. Oil shot one hundred feet or more above the crownblock and kept up a steady flow. It took some time to get the well under control and, as I remember, the first twenty-four hours' production (saved) was over two thousand barrels. The locater was elated. He had the world by the tail on a downhill pull (so he thought).

At least twenty wells were started on adjoining leases within the next few days, including one on the lease in which I was interested. Moreover, another well was started on the

Miller Farm. The results of these wells were wonderful—almost all were dry! Some very small wells were brought in, but few ever paid out.

The second well on the Miller farm was what the industry called a "stinker," just enough oil to tease you into spending money to put it pumping. The well in which I had an interest was better than the Miller well. It was no stinker. It was dry.

I never knew how the locater fared in later attempts to discover oil fields, but his first experience was disastrous to many of his contemporaries. He and his associates made a little money from the oil sold from the first well. That well declined rapidly, but did pump a few barrels for several years.

Only cable tools were used in drilling wells in those days. It was supposed that the driller had to turn the tools, and for this purpose a stick, such as a sledge handle, was fastened with a rope to the Manila cable from which the drilling bit hung. The driller would grasp the stick and walk round the hole, round and round, almost constantly, for the twelve hours of his tour.

A tour (pronounced *tower*) designates the shift worked by oil-field hands. During the early days of the industry a tour meant twelve hours' continuous work. The changes in tours were made at noon and midnight. Lease workers often put in fourteen or fifteen hours' additional work in a week, without extra pay.

Lease houses usually were provided for pumpers. Tool men had to find boardinghouses, and they drove to and from the well with a horse and buckboard. Those were in truth horse-and-buggy days. There were no paved roads in the vicinity of well locations. In spring and fall deep mud made the going so hazardous for horse-drawn vehicles that foot travel often was chosen as preferable.

Samuel M. Jones, the founder of the S. M. Jones Company and also an oil producer (as mayor of Toledo he became

14

nationally known as "Golden Rule" Jones), was, as far as I know, the first man to attempt to introduce fairer working hours on wells and leases. About 1900 he asked contractors who were drilling wells for him to run three tours of eight hours each. The contractors were willing to do this, provided they were not required to pay any more in wages than they did for two crews. The three-crew plan, on that basis, proved a failure, and the twelve-hour tour remained in vogue for many more years. Eight-hour tours now prevail in all branches of the oil industry, with overtime paid for all time worked in excess of forty hours in any one week.

While I was still a member of the Donnelly Oil Company I visited Beaumont, Tex., at the time the great Spindletop field was opened in January, 1901. I saw the famous Lucas well flow wild and was there when it was shut in. The event was far vaster than even my 28-year-old imagination could compass. Here, in fact, was the beginning of the modern petroleum industry. All that had preceded it was puny and insignificant when compared with this mammoth development.

In 1904 the Donnelly Company, having acquired from the Department of the Interior leases on certain Indian lands under suitable royalty arrangements benefitting the Osage people, drilled its first well in the Osage Nation, Indian Territory, on a lease northeast of Pawhuska. Later it drilled wells in section 2-224-R10, near the present town of Barnsdall. This was my first oil venture in what is now Oklahoma. The wells and leases were sold afterward, and the Donnelly Oil Company was dissolved.

Somewhere I have heard that, in business and industrial history at least, the study of business judgment is of the essence. It may therefore be worth while to do a short postmortem on the Donnelly undertaking. Dr. James Donnelly, the president of the company, was a practicing physician and surgeon in Toledo. The other members were J. E. Quinn, a horse-collar manufacturer of Toledo, A. K. Detweiler, a real-estate dealer, also of Toledo, Michael Donnelly, an attorney in Napoleon, Ohio, and myself.

These men had little acquaintance with the oil business, and while they had wealth and were in a position to pursue the gains they had made in the Southwest, particularly in the Osage country of the future state of Oklahoma, they did not have the venturesomeness that comes from familiarity with this type of operation. Hence their decision to sell out in 1904. The developments that were to occur in this same area would have made their investment, or an increased amount of money put at the disposal of the company in the year of its dissolution, immensely valuable.

The very locations at which the company brought in its earliest wells continued to produce in a moderate way, but the great area of the Osage Nation was still undeveloped. Had the company continued to take leases here, the oil production that was begun in that period would have continued to the present day, as subsequent pages in this account will make clear.

Now, I should say something about the Osage country, because many of my associations and operations were to take place there in the years to come.

In some senses, the Osage Indians, who in historic times had resided in Missouri, Kansas, and Arkansas, were given the biggest bonanza in the history of the United States, when the tribe was removed from its ancient hunting grounds to a portion of the Cherokee Outlet in Indian Territory after the Civil War. No one knew at the time that, beneath these lovely grass-covered hills, lay one of the great oil pools of North America. But so it was, and in two short generations the tall Osage, hunters of buffalo and ancient enemies of the Comanche in the West, were to share in vast oil wealth.

16

Their ability to profit from these developments traces to an almost unique legal provision governing their lands. Although prospecting for oil started in the Osage Nation as early as 1896, when James Bigheart, principal chief of the Osage, and Edwin B. Foster executed a lease to all of the Osage lands in behalf of Foster for a period of ten years, it was not until 1906 that Congress passed an act which reserved the mineral rights to these lands to the tribe as a whole. The act itself was concerned principally with the allotment of Osage tribal lands to individual members of the tribe, as statehood for Oklahoma approached and land in severalty became an apparent necessity in the new order of things.

But the Osage tribal representatives bargained shrewdly with Congress when they saw that individual ownership of these millions of acres could no longer be forestalled. They came away with the provision reserving the mineral rights to the tribe, and on the conclusion of the Osage tribal roll in 1907, each holder of a "head right" would in the future share equally with all other such individual members of the tribe in the income derived from the subsurface of Osage County.

It is worth remarking at this point that by 1945 these acres had produced 2 per cent of the total oil produced in the United States since 1859. It is also worth remarking that no sale whatever of portions of the surface of Osage lands can alienate the subsurface from the tribe. Many thousands of acres have passed into the hands of white ranchers and other non-members of the Osage group without disturbing the operation of this legal principle.

The Foster interests, with whom James Bigheart of the Osage had signed the blanket lease in 1896, had subleased limited areas. It was through such arrangements that the Donnelly Oil Company had undertaken some of the operations I have mentioned. Everything, however, was under the close and constant scrutiny of the Department of the Interior, Office of Indian Affairs.

In a way, the Osage development, as I experienced it in the years immediately following the turn of the century, was an extension of oil production in Kansas. Independence, Kansas, had started things off.

In the days before the oil excitement, Independence was an unobtrusive town of about thirty-five hundred population. Its chief support came from farmers living around the countryside. It had the advantage, also, of being county seat of Montgomery County. But after the Independence Gas Company began developing an oil and gas pool, which it discovered West of town, oil producers from Pennsylvania, West Virginia, Ohio, and Indiana quickly appeared.

Prairie Oil and Gas Company, which had somewhat earlier located its headquarters in Neodesha, Kansas, now moved to Independence, bringing many families with it. The Kansas Gas Company also established its main office there. Other organizations and individual operators flocked to the scene of the new oil boom. There was a scramble for homes. Population grew rapidly, and Independence, roused from its wonted composure, was soon running a fever.

Paul Bateman and I, who were among the early migrators to this area, alighted from a Missouri-Pacific train at Independence in the afternoon of February 3, 1903. We had traveled from Toledo, Ohio, where Paul was an auditor with the National Supply Company. This organization had opened supply stores in the new Midcontinent Oil Field. One of these stores was at Independence, and another at Bartlesville, Oklahoma. Paul was to be auditor for the new district. I had come to Kansas representing Donnelly, and was to obtain oil and gas leases for that company. During the past year, more and more favorable reports concerning oil in Kansas had reached Toledo, and increasing numbers of prospectors had gone to Independence and secured oil leases.

The afternoon of our arrival, Paul and I discovered that

the only hotel in Independence deserving the name was the Caldwell, run by Mr. and Mrs. Hoober, whose son Roy later was to become a vice president of the Sinclair Oil and Refining Corporation. The hotel was overcrowded, so I tried to obtain a room in a private residence. Someone told me that the T. H. Stanfords had a large home, and that two of their four boys were away at school.

I went to see Mrs. Stanford. She said that she had never taken a roomer and would not care to do so. While I was talking with her, I noticed on her piano a photograph of Professor Ewing of the University of Notre Dame. I remarked that I knew the professor quite well. That changed Mrs. Stanford's attitude immediately and I got the room.

The two Stanford boys away at school were Grattan and John. Grat later became general counsel of the Sinclair companies in New York, and John became a vice president of the Mexican companies controlled by Sinclair, with offices in Houston, Texas.

Leland (no kin to the young man in whose memory Leland Stanford, Jr. University was created) was the third son of this family, and was about fourteen at this time. He was much interested in anything that pertained to the oil business. As I gradually became part of the Stanford household, he frequently asked me to take him into the field with me. I recall that on one occasion my associates and I had a drilling well nearing completion on the Eisiminger Farm, west of Independence, and I promised to take young Leland out to see the well shot. Fulfilling my promise, I took him to the farm, but the well was not ready. The nitroglycerin shot had to be delayed because there was more sand to be drilled. I decided that we would stay at the well until all the sand and "pocket" had been drilled. This took until about three o'clock the next morning. The shooter—that is, the man who was to place and detonate the nitroglycerin necessary to get oil flowing from

19

the surrounding oil sands into the well hole—was to be back about six that morning, so it seemed better not to drive back to Independence for the short time that we would be there.

Mr. Eisiminger, the farmer, asked me to accompany him to his home. This we did, and at 5:30 that morning we had breakfast with the family. I have seen many a boy eat, but I never saw any other person, man or boy, stow away as much at one meal as Leland did then. The subsequent shooting of the well presented a sight that enthralled this youngster. Today he is a director of the Sinclair Oil Corporation in New York City.

The Independence of my first month there was a town which contained all the excitement one usually associates with oil-boom developments and at the same time many of the attractive features that Southern Kansas towns have always had, it seems to me. I was soon picking up bits of history, more interesting in the light of my oil preoccupation, perhaps, than for their value to social or cultural history as such.

I quickly discovered that McBride and Bloom, a firm of drilling contractors of Independence, had had a large hand in Kansas developments, not only at Independence, but at many other places. This firm had taken oil and gas leases on several hundred thousand acres around Cherryvale, Independence, Bolton, and Caney, and had organized the Independence Gas Company to develop and operate these leases. The company, which later changed its name to the Consolidated Oil and Gas Company, would farm out whatever acreage a prospector contracted to start drilling on. The Bolton and Wayside fields were thus opened up.

A few steps further back in history: from about 1880 to 1890, many wells were drilled in Miami County, Kansas, near the town of Paola. These wells were about three hundred feet or less in depth but did not produce much oil. In 1892, McBride and Bloom drilled a well by contract on the Norman

Farm near Neodesha. The depth was less than nine hundred feet, and the well was good for fifty barrels a day. This well was owned by a man named Mills. Mr. Mills later interested Guffey and Galey, an oil producing firm of Pittsburgh, Pennsylvania, in coming to Neodesha. Guffey and Galey took leases on several hundred thousand acres of oil land and drilled eight wells. They saw, however, that the work in Kansas would require much more money than they wished to invest there, and since they had rather large operations going at the same time in the state of their origin, Pennsylvania, they sold all their properties in Kansas to the Forest Oil Company, a subsidiary of the Standard Oil Company.

In 1897 or 1898, a refinery of five hundred barrels daily capacity was built at Neodesha by the Standard Oil Company of Kansas. This organization was a processor of much of the petroleum produced in this area in the early days. The Forest Oil Company producing properties were located principally around Neodesha, but by 1901 they were sold to the Prairie Oil and Gas Company, and in a subsequent merger of Prairie with Sinclair, about which I shall have something to say later, these properties finally came into the hands of the latter organization.

I recall that W. J. Young, of Pittsburgh, Pennsylvania, was the first president of the Prairie Oil and Gas Company. He was succeeded early in the history of the company, however, by John F. Archbold, on March 31, 1906.

My memory of these producing leases is still quite green. In fact, the equipment used was of such a character as to leave an indelible mark upon my consciousness. It was certainly varied and unique. Much of it had been home-made by the pumpers, but it all worked, and the wells actually produced. A happy sequel is that many of the wells are still producing, half a century later.

My sojourn in Independence was only a couple of years

old when an interesting development began to take shape. Early in 1905, many oil producers became dissatisfied with the treatment accorded them by the Standard Oil Company, of which Prairie Oil and Gas Company was at the time a subsidiary. Prairie was carrying through its pipe lines much of the oil produced in the area. The oil producers were mostly of two classes, those who drilled wells and produced the oil for a living, and those who sold large quantities of stock at a small price per share to public. As I remember it, most of Prairie's trouble was with the stock-selling producers. In any event, some politicians, newspapers, and interested individuals urged that the state of Kansas build an oil refinery and enter into competition with Standard Oil.

It has to be remembered that this was the period of populism, when state ownership, or socialism, in the latter-day phrase, held no terrors for many thousands of agrarians and small townsmen in the Middle West, from the Dakotas to the Gulf of Mexico. It was also the period of trust-busting and the development of public sentiment against large corporations, in which President Theodore Roosevelt had a leading role.

In any event, a war soon developed between the partisans of the state of Kansas, on the one side, and the Prairie Oil and Gas Company, on the other. Most of the newspapers in the state opposed the demand for a state owned and operated refinery.

Edward W. Hoch of Marion was elected governor, and on January 9, 1905, was sworn into office. On the same date, the legislature convened. Immediately upon the opening of that body, many plans, suggestions, and bills were offered to aid the oilmen in their fight against the Standard Oil Company.

On January 12, 1905, Senate Bill 30 was introduced by Senator Sam Porter of Montgomery County. This bill was entitled, "An Act to provide for the construction, maintenance, and operation of a state oil refinery and to provide the

22

necessary funds for such construction, maintenance, operation, and management thereof under State control." Needless to say, this bill immediately produced a large amount of activity among oilmen, either in support or in denunciation. Delegations of oilmen appeared before the legislature and the battle grew in fury.

The controversial character of this measure can partly be understood simply in terms of the liberal versus conservative tendencies of the time. The sums involved were very large, considering the fact that we had then a very hard dollar. The bill provided, for example, for an appropriation totaling two hundred thousand dollars for building a state refinery, plus ten thousand dollars for housing, feeding, and guarding the convicts to be used as its laborer force. An additional two hundred thousand dollars was appropriated for the operation of the plant, which was to be located at Peru, Chautauqua County. Governor Hoch had suggested that an experimental plant be built at Lansing, and that fifty thousand dollars be appropriated for it. However, the much more ambitious enactment envisaged in Senate Bill 30 was passed by both branches of the legislature and became law.

Then came bitter arguments regarding the validity of this act. Enough pressure was brought to bear that it was carried to the Supreme Court of Kansas for a ruling. On July 7, 1905, the Supreme Court handed down an opinion rendering Senate Bill 30 null and void.

W. S. Fitzpatrick, president of the Kansas Senate, was an opponent of the bill and made biting speeches against it when it was being considered in the Kansas legislature. Fitzpatrick was subsequently to become (in 1909) a member of the legal staff of the Prairie Oil and Gas Company, as assistant to B. F. Cates, general counsel.

3

EARLY YEARS WITH SINCLAIR

FROM THE vantage point of Independence, if one can call it that, I was operating not only in the Osage Nation, as I have already described, but in other areas of Indian Territory as well. In what was to become Nowata County in future Oklahoma, four or five of us were operating as an independent group. We put down a well near Alluwe, on the Patrick Henry Farm, but it was a duster. In subsequent years production was developed on this very lease, and it has since then all come into the fold of the Sinclair-Prairie Oil Company, with which I was soon to become associated. Such are the fortunes of the oil business.

It was in Independence that Harry F. Sinclair, who was to become a powerful figure in the oil world, started his interesting and eventful career. His home was in that city, where I too lived, and he was getting oil leases for the Cudahy Oil Company of Chicago. But he soon branched out for himself. Associated with him were John F. Overfield, A. C. Stich, and Bill Zevely, of Muskogee, Oklahoma. R. S. Litchfield and Colonel Finely, of Topeka, Kansas, joined him later.

Sinclair and I met for the first time at a social gathering in Independence, at a dance, as I recall it. He was a strongly built man then, even as now, tall, broad, with an impressive head, thin dark hair, and two piercing blue eyes.

Not many months later I found myself in association with him. I was drilling some wells for him by contract when, one day in April, 1906, I went to his office to present a bill. While I was waiting for the check, we visited. Harry asked me where my office was. I told him I had none. He said, "There is a vacant desk in the next room. You are welcome to use it." This I began doing. Harry had me do work for him, such as checking leases, drilling wells, and taking leases.

After this had gone for about four months, during which time I had used my own money for expenses, I was getting down to the bottom of my bank account. (The bottom was always close to the top in those days.) In talking over some matters with Harry one day, I asked him if I was working for him. "Sure," he replied. "Why do you ask that question?" I explained that for several months I had received no salary and no expense money. Harry expressed surprise and asked me what salary I expected. The salary question was quickly settled. He called in Ernest Huston, the office manager, and told him to have me taken care of. Thus began a relationship that has endured for almost half a century.

Among others I met in Independence were men with whom in later years I was to become associated in business. Besides Harry Sinclair and his brother Earl, who soon joined him in his enterprises, there were Ed Chandler, John Manion, Jim Flanagan, Bill O'Neill, Jim Blake, Tom Flannelly, who was Judge of the District Court at that time; Grattan, John, and Leland Stanford; Albert E. Watts, P. J. and Tom White; Nelson Moody, Sam and Horace Fitzpatrick; Ernest Huston; and many others. After retiring from the bench some years later, Tom Flannelly became general counsel for the Prairie Oil and Gas Company, and he remained in that position until the merger occurred between the Sinclair and the Prairie companies. He then became counsel for Sinclair Prairie Pipe Line Company at Independence, Kansas.

Having been brought up in the boiler and machine-shop businesses, I found friends and witnessed developments in these fields, which have from the beginning been closely associated with the oil business. Pennsylvania and Ohio were long centers of machinery and tool production, but it was remarkable how swiftly the equipment—tons of it—required for oil exploration and production was made available in a place as far from the center of things as Independence was just after the turn of the century. As activity quickened here during the oil-boom days, drilling contractors needed tools, supplies, and repair facilities—the list ran into hundreds of heavy and light pieces, from massive steel forgings to springs hardly larger than those required for a watch.

Early on the scene to meet this demand was David Bovaird, the head of Bovaird and Company, Bradford. In 1904 he built what was then considered a large shop in Independence. Bovaird had established a tool-manufacturing business in Shamburg, Pennsylvania, in 1871, later moving to Titusville, Pennsylvania, and then to Bradford. His son, William J. Bovaird, was placed in charge of the Independence shop. Jim Flanagan was made office manager.

The firm later incorporated as the Bovaird Supply Company, with William J. Bovaird as president. Its first supply store was opened in Sapulpa, Oklahoma. Flanagan went to Sapulpa as secretary-treasurer of the company. William J. Bovaird remained in Independence, and shortly before his death in 1937 his son Mervin Bovaird succeeded him as president. The company now has stores in oil fields of Oklahoma, Kansas, and Texas, and is still growing. Its general headquarters are in Tulsa.

Following Mervin's death in 1949, his brother Davis D. Bovaird, was made president. Davis's son, William J.

Bovaird II, is assistant to the general manager of stores. His son, William J. Bovaird III, is a lusty young man of 4 years who gives every promise of helping to maintain the family's high place in the oil industry. I feel quite ancient when I contemplate how I have known five generations of the Bovaird family.

At about the same time that the Bovaird Company entered Kansas, the Independence Iron Works opened a machine shop. This company was owned by John Finley, of Lima, Ohio. Patsy Mack, one of the best known oil-country machinists, was placed in charge. W. D. (Bill) O'Neill, of Lima, was secretary-treasurer. The drilling of wells moved south into Oklahoma. Finley died, and this concern lost business and closed up. O'Neill, who had previously been an oil correspondent for the Oil City (Pa.) *Derrick,* a Pat Boyle publication, then joined Boyle when the latter established the *Oil and Gas Journal* in Tulsa.

The largest corporation supplying mechanical needs of the oil industry is the National Supply Company, organized in Ohio as the Buckeye Oil Well Supply Company. W. M. Hillman, experienced as a supply man in Pennsylvania, induced Shaw, Kendall and Company, who dealt in plumbing supplies, to join him in establishing the Buckeye company. Its first store was opened at Cygnet, Ohio, where big wells were many. The name of the company was later changed to National Supply Company. This corporation has had a phenomenal growth and now has branch stores and many large manufacturing plants in all of the oil states. It also has branches in foreign lands. I mention this company because I have known it from its birth. I also knew Shaw, Kendall, Hardee, Hillman, and Wolcott, founders of the corporation. I have done business with the firm for over fifty years.

The Continental Supply Company, a subsidiary of the Youngstown Sheet & Tube Company, was organized in 1912.

Alf Heggam, its first president, was succeeded by W. K. Hughes, who in turn was succeeded by H. B. Gutelius. Officers now are W. J. Morris, chairman of board; F. M. Mayer, president; F. I. Brinegar, vice-president. Continental is one of the really important supply companies in the industry.

After leaving Continental, Gutelius organized his own concern under the name of United Supply and Manufacturing Company, and he has built up a large and substantial following among producers and oil-well contractors.

Some months before my formal association with Harry F. Sinclair began, I was able to witness another of the great events connected with the history of petroleum development in North America. In November, 1905, the greatest strike up to that time, in Oklahoma at least, was made at Glenn Pool by Robert Galbraith and Frank Chesley. Quickly, I found myself becoming interested in that area, where I succeeded in getting some leases.

Many of us said at the time (and we were pretty far wrong), "There will never be another pool like this one." It was prodigious. Oil was found at a relatively shallow depth, where it was easy to produce, and the horror of it was that there wasn't enough pipe-line capacity at the time to take care of the production. The idea of shutting in production in those days was a nightmare. It was generally assumed that if a well was choked back or cut off entirely, even for a period of hours, it might be ruined. This has subsequently been proved to be nonsense, as all oilmen know, but a great many of the now accepted engineering facts were not available to us when the oil business was young.

In the wide world of developing oil activity, I suppose Glenn Pool may serve as an example of what was going on, although admittedly the pool was a good deal more sensational than most that were developed in the period from 1900 to 1910. It was discovered in fairly open country, with a slight roll to it, and the discovery well went to a depth of only a little over fourteen hundred feet. Most of the subsequent production, however, was from the Bartlesville Sand, which is somewhat deeper and dipping to the west. There was no clearly defined well-spacing in that era, except insofar as an operator or company chose to utilize the principle of putting wells far enough apart to get maximum recovery from the oil sands.

Wooden derricks, then used almost universally in the oil fields, could be constructed, and the cable drilling tools got into operation, in five or six days. Going to a depth of fourteen hundred to two thousand feet in that area required only another eighteen to twenty days, if my memory serves me right. Quickly a locality which had been strictly rural began to mushroom. Wells were drilled on seven- or eight-acre spacing, with variations, because there were many leases in the field, until the whole countryside had a bristling appearance from the hundreds of wooden derricks rising to the sky. There were as many as fifty to one hundred wells drilling at a given time, and, of course, hundreds of earlier wells, also with their derricks, producing the oil pool that had already been tapped.

The whole scene was made eerie at night by scores of visible gas flares. At that time, we used as much of the gas produced by a given well as we might need for fuel purposes on the location, and the rest was flared, that is, lighted and allowed to burn indefinitely. This was so because the pools were developed very fast, and there were really no marketing facilities for the natural gas thus produced.

Moreover, this was the period before the advent of gasoline plants, which were to convert natural gas into motor fuels. It is easy to look back and call this wastefulness, just as it is possible to make similar assessments of such industries as mining, farming, lumbering, and railroading in their earlier days. The chemical and engineering accomplishments which were later to utilize every cubic foot of natural gas and gallon of oil for the production of an infinite number of by-products, as well as lubricants and fuels, had yet to be approached even at the laboratory stage.

It is easily possible in this part of my story to overlook chronology, which I do not wish to do. On the other hand, I can explain the gigantic character of oil development at the time only by telescoping a good many phases, some of which I had the good fortune to witness in the decade or more after the opening of Glenn Pool.

It was like a series of fingers extending down from the Kansas country into the Osage Nation, into future Nowata County, south into future Tulsa County, south again to Glenn Pool and Creek County; while westward, the fingers extended to Garber in Garfield County, south and westward into the Ponca City area, down to Healdton, and by a wide half-moon over into Cushing, Drumright, Bald Hill, and other areas.

We followed, or tried to follow, all of the leads that new drilling turned up for us. We followed the trend until it played out. Gradually, the production which had begun in a hesitant way in Kansas and northern Oklahoma spread ever southward, while simultaneously that which had begun in southern Texas extended itself northward, and the two sets of fingers were to meet at the Red River separating the two states.

All along the lines of this development were boom towns galore. There was frantic movement of oil field equipment over roads that had seen no paving. Much of the equipment was moved by teams rather than by power-driven trucks. Oil was money, and the scramble for it was earnest and relentless. Men learned to snatch sleep where they could get it. Meals were taken at boarding houses, at cheap restaurants, in a sack from a grocery store, in fact, wherever it could be got, and the cost was almost never small.

The whole character of this activity has to be understood in terms of slow transportation, for the automobile and the truck, although they were already with us, came equipped with tires which were easily blown out on the rough roads. Heavy traffic in producing areas created road blocks in the form of rutting that kept everything at a snail's pace. Men consequently had to be away from home for long periods of time, and although the boom towns developed rapidly, they did not offer a solution to the home and housing problem that might be supposed. For oil development was then and forever beyond the next hill, and the whole industry literally moved across the countryside from month to month.

There were times when I wondered about the purpose of all our straining activity. Some of the automobiles then in vogue could hardly have been the cause of it. For example: One day while living in Independence, I had to make a trip to Bartlesville, Oklahoma. The business in hand required an attorney, so I took R. W. (Bob) Kellough with me. We started off in my E. M. F. automobile. About a mile out of Dewey the car quit.

We got out, and for two hours I worked over the machine's innards, pulling out this, pushing in that, turning something else. Bob meanwhile, being a lawyer, bestrewed advice copiously. At last I got the engine running. Triumphantly I wiped some of the grease off my hands and got behind the wheel.

I threw in the clutch, applied the gas, and we began moving BACKWARD! I tried all the gear shifts in the book. The result was always the same. The machine made a joyous leap to the rear every time. Bob hinted that we might just head the car for Independence and thus reach Bartlesville. I treated the suggestion with the contempt it deserved.

Finally, after diving into the ditch twice, we left the car where it was and walked to Dewey, where we hired a livery rig and drove to Bartlesville. There we sent out a car to haul in my machine for repairs.

31

Shortly after I had become "formally" associated with Harry Sinclair and Glenn Pool was getting under way, we acquired a lease on an allotment near Sapulpa. It was a piece of Indian land, the surface to which had been leased by a white farmer. We were ready to move in, but the farmer demanded much higher damages than we believed we should pay for the right to move across his land with our equipment and set up a well location.

Howard Galbreath, one of our superintendents, went to Sapulpa and tried to effect a settlement of the dispute with the farmer. He got exactly nowhere. Harry Sinclair then sent me down from our office in Independence to give Howard a hand. We adopted a course of action which looked promising. Teams hauling rig timbers were to be sent to the lease. Howard and I would follow in a buckboard, driving at a rate that would allow us to overtake the teams a few minutes after they reached the lease.

The teams were at the lease, as we planned, when we drove up. The farmer was sitting on a chair just inside the gate with a businesslike expression on his face and a still more businesslike rifle across his knees.

With the air of one in unquestionable command of the situation, I dropped from the buckboard and walked to the gate. Keeping my eyes off the rifle as much as possible, I delivered a dignified address. It was a masterful presentation of our case, closing with a forceful demand that we be permitted to enter.

The farmer eyed me with stony composure. His response to my speech was an unqualified "No!" to which he added a concise appendix to the effect that he would shoot any white-liver so-and-so who tried to pass him.

I forthwith opened the gate, and with a gesture that meant I would stand for no nonsense, I told the teamster in the lead to drive in.

32

"Not on your life!" he replied.

"Well, get down then," I snapped. He obeyed with alacrity.

With something of that high valor which glued the youthful Casabianca to the burning deck whence all but him had fled, I mounted the seat and sharply ordered, "Giddap!"

The horses barely had their heads past the gateposts when the farmer rasped a strident "Whoa!" The team stopped. The farmer strolled over to the wagon, jabbed the muzzle of the rifle against my midriff, and growled "Now, you lousy thus-and-so, if you drive an inch farther I'll drill a hole through you!" Giving the rifle a vicious poke, he mumbled an insulting epithet which reflected upon my parentage.

I was profoundly impressed by his words and manner. So was Howard, who shouted, "Get down, Billy! for God's sake, get down!"

I was already down.

Howard and I drove to Sapulpa and conferred with the Indian agent there. Accompanied by a policeman from the Indian Agency, we returned to the lease, where, under the protection of the officer, we moved our rig onto the location.

When I recounted our experience to Sinclair, he said, "He wouldn't have shot you. Why didn't you go on in?"

"Well," I replied, "that rifle looked a lot bigger when it was shoved into my anatomy than it could look from the office here in Independence, one hundred miles away."

And to this day I believe that farmer was a man of his word.

The present size and elaboration of oil companies are apt to obscure the condition of things in an earlier time. A company president of a half century ago was very accessible for personal interview or conversation by local or long-distance telephone. This was owing to the strength of an adage, even then of long and reputable standing in the oil industry, to the effect that "oil and gas are where you find them." A successful oil man had to be alert and responsive to any lead whatever that might give him a chance at new production.

Sinclair one day received a long-distance telephone call from a Mr. Green, in Dalhart, Texas, who wanted a capable man sent to Dalhart at once to investigate a "gas find." Green agreed to have two hundred dollars deposited in an Independence bank to cover the cost of the investigation. He did not want his gas discovery to become generally known and asked that the man sent to Dalhart use a fictitious name and give Kansas City as his address in registering at a hotel. I was assigned to the job.

I arrived in Dalhart at about 4:30 A. M. during a blizzard, went to a hotel, and got to bed immediately. At about 7 o'clock I was awakened by Green, who announced that he was ready. I called attention to the storm, but he said that wouldn't interfere because the gas field was only a block or so from the hotel.

After breakfast Green escorted me to a men's furnishing store on the main street, near the hotel. He explained that he had only recently purchased the place and furnished it as a haberdashery. A restaurant had been conducted there previously. The cook formerly had worked in Cherryvale, Kansas, and thus was familiar with gas as a fuel.

One evening as the restaurant was about to close, the dishwasher struck a match in the kitchen and there was an explosion. The dishwasher was badly burned. Green usually ate his meals in the restaurant, and the cook convinced him that there was a gas field under the building. So Green bought the place, closed the restaurant, and installed the haberdashery. At the rear was a cesspool. Green told me that he had run a half-inch pipe from this cesspool to the kitchen and had obtained enough gas through it to boil an egg.

We put some snow (there was plenty of that around) and two eggs in a small pail and opened the door of the kitchen.

34

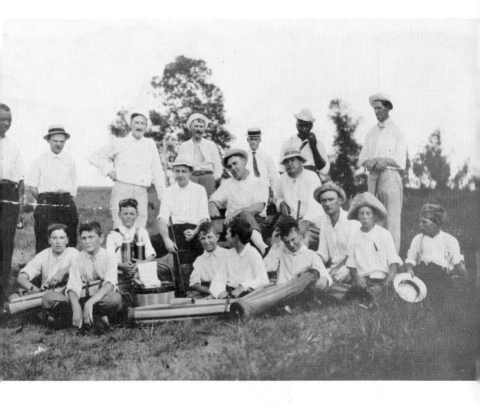

Golf at the Independence, Kansas, Country Club, 1910. *Top row, left to right:* Pink White, Fritz Wilhelm, C. A. McAdams, E. T. Patterson, W. A. Love, Ike Montgomery, E. W. Sinclair. *Middle row:* J. B. Robinson, W. F. Gates, H. F. Sinclair. James McCleland, and caddies.

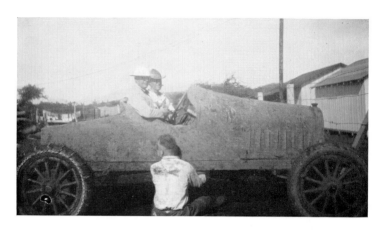

Oil field travel, Mexico, 1918—the roads were rough.

The *Claro,* a noble launch until she burned.

There was no sign of any gas. We hung the pail on Green's pipe, applied a lighted match to the end of the pipe, and waited for gas to ignite. Nothing doing. We went out into the yard and investigated the cesspool. No gas.

I decided that gas had accumulated in the pool and, through a leak in the floor, had entered the kitchen, igniting and causing the explosion. After the restaurant had been closed, no more grease was dumped into the cesspool, so no more gas was formed. I went back to Independence. Thus was added another to the long list of disappointments in the gas business.

4

CHASING A CHEROKEE

MUCH HAS BEEN written about the vanishing Indian since the white man took over in this country. One Indian's proficiency in the art of vanishing afforded an exciting experience that exhausted all my resources of strategy, ingenuity, and persistence. Stealthy pursuit, sly escapes, a special train chartered in an emergency—these were among features of a memorable battle of wits in which an oil lease was the prize awaiting the winner. My campaign developed a thrilling man hunt which came to be referred to as "Chasing a Cherokee."

In the fall of 1906, the region embraced by future Nowata County, Oklahoma, was a scene of active exploratory drilling. Good wells were being brought in, and there was an avid quest for leases. I found that Frank Tanner, a 20-year-old Cherokee Indian, had an allotment of 110 acres in a 160-acre tract which was looked upon as a particularly promising spot. A short-term lease on the Tanner property, held by Theodore Barnsdall, would expire when Tanner became of age on February 14, 1908. Barnsdall had not drilled because there was no assurance that his lease would be renewed when Tanner attained his majority.

Individual Indian land holdings, as I have said earlier in

connection with the Osage, were relatively new to members of the tribes residing in Indian Territory. For this and other reasons, a considerable amount of supervision was given these Indian land holders by the U.S. Indian Office, Department of the Interior. Thus, a lease on an Indian minor's allotment could be sold by a master in chancery, and the lease would remain in force until the minor had reached his majority, at which time it was cancelled automatically. He could then make a lease on his own terms to anybody of his choice.

This applied particularly to Indians of the Five Civilized Tribes—Cherokees, Choctaws, Creeks, Chickasaws, and Seminoles—of eastern, northern, and southern Oklahoma. In this these tribesmen differed from the Osage, the subsurface values in whose lands were held in common by the Osage Tribe, as previously outlined.

Perhaps I should explain also that lease terms for oil production were then, and remain now, rather standard. The customary royalty terms provided that a lease holder should receive one-eighth of the sums realized from the production of oil from the area under lease by an oil producing company. Added financial benefits to the lease holder were not uncommon, however. A bonus might be paid, for example, to the lease holder on his signing a lease agreement. This could be anywhere from fifty cents an acre to eighteen hundred or two thousand dollars an acre—even more. Sometimes an overriding arrangement was allowed whereby the lease holder would receive the first several hundred or several thousand barrels of production of oil, and thereafter receive the customary one-eighth.

The important points to remember about Tanner and his lease are, that he was within months of attaining his majority, when the lease previously held by Barnsdall might or might not be renewed by Tanner when he attained the age of 21; and that the game was essentially a struggle between two oil organizations to produce oil on Tanner's property. Under prevailing lease and bonus arrangements, Tanner himself stood only to gain.

I looked up the young Cherokee with a view of persuading him to make a lease to us. I offered him a bonus of twenty thousand dollars with the stipulation that until the lease should be approved by the Secretary of the Interior we were to give him one hundred dollars a month toward payment of the bonus. Upon such approval, the remainder of the twenty thousand dollars was to be paid. He accepted this proposition. I took him to the office of W. D. Humphrey, a lawyer, and we signed an agreement closing the trade. I knew that the contract was not enforceable, but thought that it might impress Tanner. Many others besides me were dogging the young Indian, and I had difficulty holding him in line, but the bonus was no small prize.

I found out that Tanner was a baseball player and a promising pitcher. Harry Sinclair owned the Independence Baseball Club at that time, and he agreed with me that if Tanner were signed as a pitcher for the next season's team it probably would help us in our efforts to land that lease. Tanner signed up and was satisfied for a short time, but began to get nervous again.

Fred Clarke, who managed the Pittsburgh Pirates in the National League, lived at Akron, Kansas, near Winfield. I had met Clarke previously and now arranged to meet him in Winfield on the next Saturday. I explained our case to him, and he agreed to take Tanner on the training trip with the Pirates, we to pay Tanner's expenses; but we had failed to keep in mind that the trip would not start until March, so that was out.

I persuaded Clarke to write Tanner explaining that I had urged him to give the Indian a chance to break into the big league. The letter was to say that if Tanner put up a good performance with Independence in 1908 Clarke would give him a tryout the next spring. Tanner received the letter and proudly showed it around Nowata. I felt that we were making progress, but realized there must be no letup until the lease was actually in hand.

Earl Weible, who owned a furnishing store in Nowata, was a friend of Tanner's. He was to leave for Chicago the latter part of January to buy his spring stock. Earl agreed to take Tanner on the trip. I was to meet them in Chicago and try to have the lease signed there while Tanner was away from distracting influences. For some reason the trip was called off. This was a setback, so I had to intensify my campaigning.

John Payne of Oil City, Pennsylvania, who had an oil lease on the Pyburn twenty-acre piece which adjoined Tanner's place, planned to start a well on it in four or five weeks. I induced him to start within two weeks by agreeing to pay for the drilling. If the well should prove a dry hole, I could abandon my chase after Tanner.

During the week preceding February 14, Sinclair had gone east. He was to stop in Pittsburgh on his way home and ask John A. Bell, Sr., to put up the twenty-thousand-dollar bonus which had been promised Tanner and take an interest in the lease. Bell, a banker and oilman, was a friend of Sinclair's. Sinclair was to advise me when the arrangement with Bell had been completed. But in his conference with Sinclair, Bell was unable to name the exact day on which he could have the bonus ready or even give positive assurance that he would provide it. He said he would wire Sinclair his decision the following day while Sinclair was on the train.

In the meantime, I had secured from Charles and Ida Tanner, Frank's parents, affidavits that Frank's birth date was February 14. This was done to protect us on that point.

Sinclair arrived in Independence on a Sunday morning. He told me then that while he was in the Union Depot at St.

Louis he had received a wire from Bell to the effect that the latter would go along on the deal.

I left Independence Sunday afternoon for Nowata to see Tanner. I could not find him in any of his usual haunts, and I feared someone had "stolen" him. While I was sitting on the porch at the Carey Hotel, McConnell Elder, an oilman, stopped there for a few minutes. He was carrying a grip, which made me feel that he had been trying to persuade Tanner to lease to him. I was immediately suspicious that Elder had spirited Tanner away and was on his way to the hide-out.

When Elder got on a late train for the north, I was right after him, and when he got off the train at Coffeyville, I followed. He took a hack, and I heard him tell the driver to go to the Mecca Hotel. I followed in another hack but waited outside the hotel until Elder had registered. Then I went in and registered. I noted that Elder had been assigned Room 32, say. I needed to know if Elder had left a call and for what hour. There was no elevator in the hotel, and as I started up the stairs I stopped and called back to the clerk, asking him to call 32 (Elder's room) at 6:30.

The clerk looked at his card and said, "I have a call for that room at 7, but it is not your room."

I apologized for momentarily "forgetting" my room number. In the morning I was in the lobby when Elder came down. He went into the dining room and I followed shortly. When he left the hotel he went to a lawyer's office. I could not follow him into the office, but thinking Tanner might be at his parent's home, I went there. Mrs. Tanner said that Frank had been at the house the evening before, but that he was taking a trip some place with Joe Rogers, a pal.

I went back to Coffeyville and after persistent investigation found the hack driver who had driven Tanner and Rogers to the Katy Railroad station that morning. They had bought tickets for Guthrie. I called Sinclair and told him the story of my devious travels. "Come on home," he said. "You have lost Tanner."

"No," I replied; "you call Mrs. Connelly. Have her pack a grip for me and give it to a conductor on the Interurban Railway. I'll pick up the grip and go to Guthrie."

I took a train out of Coffeyville twenty-four hours after my quarry had gone. I had been up since 6 o'clock that morning and was tired and worried. I went to bed with instructions to the Pullman conductor to call me in time to be up when we reached Osage Junction, where Katy trains for Tulsa left the branch line and took the main line. Osage Junction was also an eating place for train passengers. I thought Tanner and Rogers might have left Guthrie and be heading for Tulsa.

On getting back on the train after eating breakfast, I cautioned the conductor not to fail to awaken me in case I should fall asleep. I did not go back to bed. The train was bound for Oklahoma City, and it was necessary to change cars for Guthrie at Fallis. I woke up from a doze just as the train was pulling into Oklahoma City. The conductor had failed me.

While waiting twenty minutes for a train back to Fallis, I called on Tom Boland, an old friend of mine, who was with a wholesale grocery company. Its plant was close to the depot. I found Tom and asked him to check the hotels for Tanner and Rogers and to call me at Guthrie if he learned anything about them.

On arriving at Guthrie I went to the Ione Hotel. There I was told that the objects of my hunt had checked out the evening before and were on their way to Denver. This was a stunner. I knew only one man in Denver, an attorney. I called him and told him enough of my story to arouse his interest. He agreed to have Tanner picked up by the police on some holding charge and detained until I could reach Denver.

I scarcely had left the telephone booth when I was called back. Boland was on the line. He had located Tanner and

Rogers in Oklahoma City. They were with Charles J. Wrightsman and Gene Blaize, two well-known and smart oil producers. I knew then that I had a real fight ahead. Boland agreed to keep track of Tanner as well as he could. I was to get to Oklahoma City by rail as soon as possible, which would be early in the evening. There were no taxicabs available.

Boland met me at the Oklahoma City station and told me that he had followed Wrightsman and Blaize until Wrightsman called a policeman and had him taken into custody. Boland was released at the police station, and he at once resumed his chase. He found Wrightsman and Blaize at the Huckins Hotel.

Tanner and Rogers were in a rooming house on Main Street. Boland had a friend who ran an all-night restaurant directly across the street from the rooming house. Boland and I went to see his friend. I obtained permission to use a seat at the desk in the front part of the restaurant whenever I wished.

I went to the Threadgill Hotel for a few hours' sleep, and at 7 o'clock the next morning I was at the desk. At about 9 o'clock the two boys came over to the restaurant and sat down for their breakfasts. I left the desk, went outside, and stood in a doorway to wait and watch. When the two came out they walked to the Huckins Hotel and separated. Rogers went upstairs, presumably to report to Wrightsman and Blaize. Tanner went to the washroom, where I joined him. He began to explain how he happened to be in Oklahoma City. I cut him short by telling him that Fred Clarke wanted me to bring him to Pittsburgh at once.

Tanner was elated, but said that he had no money and no good clothes. I told him that I could furnish the money (I had about forty dollars with me), and that we would get some "real clothes" in Pittsburgh. He agreed to go with me but wanted to tell Rogers where he was going. I talked him out

42

of that. We bought tickets for Coffeyville, where I intended to take the Interurban to Independence. It was my plan to meet Sinclair there and after midnight of February 14 to close the lease deal, giving Tanner what was still due on the bonus.

About four minutes before the train left, Wrightsman and Blaize, with Rogers, drove up to the station in a Thomas Flyer, one of the fastest automobiles of that day. They came into the car, picked Tanner up bodily, carried him to their car and rode off. The car was driven by a fifth man, whom we did not recognize.

This was a body blow. I feared that I was licked. I went over to see Boland, and we speculated as to where the Thomas Flyer would go. There were no paved roads and few garages in that period. We figured that the fleeing men would stick to the bigger towns. I called the police of Shawnee, El Reno, and several other towns and told them it was vital that we locate the car, owing to an emergency affecting one of the men in it.

At noon I called Sinclair by the telephone, knowing he usually arrived at his office in Independence about that time. I explained the case to him. "You can handle Blaize," he said, "but Wrightsman is too fast for you. I'll go down to Oklahoma City and join you."

Sinclair arrived in Oklahoma City about 10 o'clock that evening. I met him at the station and brought him up to the minute on what had taken place. I had spent a busy afternoon. I had found out that the Thomas Flyer was owned and driven by Oscar Dick, who kept it in a small garage in the city. I went to this garage at about 7 o'clock and told the man in charge that I had to know where Dick would be that night; that if he could obtain this information I would give him twenty dollars. As a guarantee I cut a twenty-dollar bill in two, gave him one-half and promised that the other half would be given to him as soon as he provided the desired information concerning Dick's whereabouts.

At about 9 o'clock he called me at the hotel and said that he had news for me. I hurried to the garage. Dick had telephoned that his party would be at Hennessey that night, but he did not know where they would go the next day. I surrendered my half of the twenty-dollar bill and left.

Upon Sinclair's arrival he said that until I had phoned him he had no idea we were in a battle with Wrightsman, that Wrightsman was a clever man, and that if we outwitted him we would have to go some. He first scouted the idea that the car was at Hennessey, but when I called attention to the fact that the garage man had known who was with Dick, he agreed that it might be true. We went to the Huckins Hotel, where Sinclair registered. After we had reached his room he said, "We might find out if that car is at Hennessey by calling the night marshal." This we did, but the marshal reported no soap. I then left for my hotel.

I was just getting into bed when the phone rang. Sinclair said that the marshal at Hennessey had called him to say that the four were in Hennessey. The question now was where they might go from there. I pointed out that Enid was about 20 miles north of Hennessey and that Guthrie was southeast; that Enid could not be reached quickly by rail, but that a train for Guthrie would be along soon. "Let's go!" exclaimed Sinclair.

We had about fifteen minutes to catch the train. I finished dressing in the cab on the way to the station. At Guthrie we spent a few hours in bed. Lieutenant Governor Bellamy, who resided in Guthrie, owned one of the few autos in Oklahoma. Through some wire-pulling, Sinclair achieved the loan of the Lieutenant Governor's car and driver and had the car parked in front of the hotel. We thought that Wrightsman and Blaize might come through Guthrie, and that if they did and we saw them (a long chance), we would use the Bellamy car to follow them. In the meantime I was busy on the phone trying to

44

locate the Thomas Flyer for the "emergency message" that I said I had for Tanner.

Sometime in the afternoon Chief of Police Al Thrasher at Enid called me and said, "Your people are here, but I don't know whether they will stay here tonight or try to go into Guthrie. As soon as I hear what they intend to do I'll call again."

So, once more I gnawed my fingernails and walked ten miles around the hotel lobby. If Wrightsman and his party were coming to Guthrie, Sinclair and I could act as a reception committee, but if they stayed in Enid, we had to get there. About 5 o'clock Chief Thrasher called with news that on account of the rain (it had been raining at intervals all day) the Wrightsman party would stay in Enid.

In oil-country parlance, we were in "one hell of a fix." The last train for Enid that day had already left. We were afraid to try to drive to Enid in the Bellamy car, owing to the rain, the muddy roads, and the darkness. Our only alternative was to hire a special train. But we had no money.

While we were trying to figure that one out, Charles Owen of Caney, Kansas, came into the hotel. He was a friend of both of us. Sinclair braced him for some money. Owen had only about twenty-five dollars in cash, but he had a draft for two hundred dollars. This draft he gave to Sinclair. I went to the Santa Fe station with it and arranged for a special train from Guthrie to Enid. The agent agreed to take the pay for the train, eighty-five dollars, out of the draft.

At 7 o'clock Sinclair and I were at the station. Our train, consisting of an engine, baggage car, and a coach, was on the track ready to go, but the agent had changed his mind about accepting the draft. Sinclair argued—and he can do a good job as an arguer—but the agent was adamant. We went back to the hotel to cash the draft, but the cashier did not have enough money on hand to help us. The owner of the hotel was

45

in his room, suffering from a bad cold, but after Sinclair explained our situation, he cashed the draft.

Back we went to the station, but during our absence the agent had dismissed the crew. By the time the train was ready again it was almost midnight.

I have the receipt for the payment for the train in front of me as I write this. It is written on an Atchison, Topeka & Santa Fe Railway form No. 201 and reads: "Received of W. L. Connelly, eighty-five dollars ($85.00) for one ticket from Guthrie to Enid Form 60— Number 27345 via special train. N. Cochrell, Agent." It is stamped "February 13, 1908."

While we were held up by the train mix-up, I had again called Chief Thrasher at Enid and asked him to meet us at the station there. When we arrived at Enid early in the morning of February 14, the chief met us. He said that Wrightsman was at the Lowden Hotel and that Blaize and the two boys were in a small hotel at the edge of the city. He agreed to try to have Tanner in his office early in the morning and to hold him there until he heard from me.

Sinclair and I went to the Lowden, arranged for our rooms, and then called on Wrightsman. This was about 2 o'clock in the morning. Wrightsman was utterly dumbfounded when he saw us. "I thought I left you at the Katy station in Oklahoma City," he said to me. I agreed that this was where he had seen me last but added that I had moved around some. He wanted to know how I had found him. I divulged nothing, but since then I have told him the whole story. Wrightsman and I, ever since that night, have been close friends, and the company has made many trades with him. He is still active in business and is located in Fort Worth, Texas.

Wrightsman invited us into his room, and we proceeded to discuss the Tanner lease. After we had argued for an hour or more and made no progress, Wrightsman suggested that we meet again at 10 o'clock that morning, giving us his word

46

that he would make no move in the interim. This suited me exactly, for I needed sleep.

At about 8 o'clock that morning Chief Thrasher called me to say that Tanner was with him at his office ready for us. In accordance with the agreement made the day before, Wrightsman and Blaize came to Sinclair's room at 10 o'clock, and we resumed our discussion. Sinclair proposed that a fair settlement would be for Wrightsman and Blaize to have a one-half interest in the lease and we the other half. Wrightsman and Blaize proposed that they take 75 per cent and we 25 per cent. No deal. Wrightsman then suggested a 66⅔ and 33⅓ per cent division. Sinclair replied that he would take 50 per cent or the entire interest. Wrightsman and Blaize had a hearty laugh. Thereupon I called the chief of police and asked him to bring Frank to our room. Wrightsman and Blaize were astounded.

Within 10 minutes Frank Tanner was in our room. Coming directly to me he declared, "I want you to have my lease." That settled the whole business.

Sinclair and Wrightsman that afternoon formed a new company. That the tense weeks through which we had passed had left no bitterness and had spoiled neither man's sense of humor is evidenced by the name they gave the new organization, the Chaser Oil Company, one-half of the stock being owned by Wrightsman and Blaize, the other half being owned by Sinclair, Bell and myself.

I went to Nowata and had John Payne drill in the Pyburn well, which came in for about 500 barrels at 630 feet.

Tanner was given what was due on his twenty-thousand-dollar bonus, but he never became a big-league pitcher. The Chaser Oil Company drilled six or eight wells on the Tanner lease, each good for four hundred to six hundred barrels. We sold our half interest to the Prairie Oil and Gas Company. Wrightsman and Blaize later sold their half to the same company.

Twenty-five years later, in 1932, at the time of the merger of the Prairie Oil and Gas Company with the Sinclair Oil and Gas Company, this lease came back home. During the life of this lease until December 31, 1950, it had produced under primary and gas repressuring a total of about 1,300,000 barrels, and after forty-four years it is still producing more than thirty barrels daily. We are now arranging to start a water-flood project which I believe will yield an additional 700,000 to 750,000 barrels of oil under this relatively new method devised by engineers for revitalizing old fields.

This episode of the oil country has been written up many times, but the persons participating in it have never before been named correctly. Following this lease transaction came another one covering the Clyde, Albert, Lillie, and Zoma Tanner allotments. All of these allotments had been leased to Jennings Brothers and John A. Bell, Sr. The leases were about to expire, and the holders were having difficulty in getting them extended.

Roger Kemp was in charge of the Jennings and Bell interests in Oklahoma. He sent several leasemen to try to get the leases. None was successful. Then Roger himself tried it. No better results. A law firm of Bartlesville, Oklahoma, Veasey and Rowland, then took over. They had no better luck.

I had the answer. Mr. and Mrs. Tanner were taking my advice on what they should do. I had told Sinclair that I could get these leases for him. He would not listen. He said that John Bell was a partner of his and that he would have no hand in taking Bell's leases away from him. Sinclair finally agreed that if the others failed to make a deal with Tanner I could do my bit. I was elated at that decision. I knew that the Jennings brothers and Bell would never get the leases. Bell and his son, John A. Bell, Jr., came out from Pittsburgh and got into the trade themselves, but Tanner still was immovable.

The Bells finally decided that they were licked. They planned to go back to Pittsburgh, stopping off at Independence to visit Sinclair en route. This was my undoing.

During the visit the elder Bell said he had been much disappointed over his inability to make the Tanner trade. He asked Sinclair if he could help.

Sinclair said, "I can't, but there is a man in the next room who can." He called me into his office and said, "Billy, I want you to go to Coffeyville with Mr. Bell and help him get the Tanner leases."

That was a blow to me. I had counted confidently on getting these leases for Sinclair. I gulped a few times and said "O.K." We met with Jim Veasey, of Veasey and Rowland, the next morning in Coffeyville to discuss ways of handling the trades. I could tell that he had no idea that I would be able to do what a dozen high-powered landmen, Roger Kemp, the Bells, Rowland, and Veasey himself had failed at.

We had made an engagement with the Tanners for the afternoon. I insisted that I do the talking with them. For once I was giving orders to bankers and lawyers. We came away with the deal all settled. I never made a deal in my life that afforded me less pleasure than this one. I was cutting my own throat every time I urged Tanner to close the trade. The only person in the group who sensed my feelings was Jim Veasey. He seemed to understand what a strain I was under. Many times since then Jim and I have discussed what took place that afternoon, and he has been lavish in his compliments. Each compliment is a grain of salt in the wound of a lost cause!

The Jennings brothers and Bell, after drilling a number of wells on these leases, sold the leases to the Prairie Oil and Gas Company. In 1932, at the time of the Sinclair-Prairie merger, they came back to the Sinclair Prairie Oil Company. They will be in the group that will be under the water-flood, along with the Frank Tanner and other leases in the Childers area, looking to a large volume of secondary recovery of oil.

Sinclair certainly was Santa Claus's little helper (for the Jennings brothers and Bells) that afternoon. Tanner and his estate realized nearly $250,000 in the next forty-five years, and under the water-flooding now begun, he and his heirs should realize another $100,000 to $125,000.

Me? I was only the chaser.

But there are other ways of wasting time—and losing money.

Some time before we moved our offices from Independence to Tulsa, Harry Sinclair asked me to discuss with Tom Flannelly, judge of the District Court, the merits of the younger members of the Montgomery County bar, and to get the Judge to name three of the most capable among them. The Judge recommended the following in the order given: Edward H. Chandler, Grattan T. Stanford, and Oscar O'Brien. Harry asked me to have Ed Chandler come to the office. Ed came over. Harry explained that we were about to move our offices to Tulsa, that he needed a full-time attorney, and that he would like to have Ed join the organization. As a result of this conference Ed joined us on January 1, 1913.

Before we moved to Tulsa a lease broker telephoned Harry that he had found "Joe Buckskin" (not his real name), a full-blood Creek who had an allotment which had never been leased for the reason that "Joe" had disappeared. The allotment looked good for oil. This broker said he had "Joe" in Muskogee and that he could get a lease on the allotment for Harry. The price for the lease and the broker's services and expenses would be twenty thousand dollars in cash—no drafts or checks.

"Go to Muskogee," Harry directed me, "and if things are

Tankers loading at docks in the Panuco River, Mexico, 1918.

Freeport Mexican Oil Company well on Guiterrez Farm, Panuco, Mexico, flowing 8,000 barrels per day into earthen tanks, 1918. This well was located not as a normal offset, but close to water. The later, normally placed wells were small ones. Maybe I was lucky.

Sinclair Mexican Oil Corporation well on Lot 251, Amatlan, Mexico, 1920; maximum production, 70,000 barrels per day.

O. K. take the lease, but be sure that you have the real Joe."
This caution was prompted by the fact that many leases had
been given by phony owners.

"Maybe you had better take Ed Chandler with you,"
Harry added. "He may as well get into these deals now."

Ed and I took twenty thousand dollars in cash and left for
Muskogee. The broker, whom I knew only slightly, met us at
the Katy Hotel. He had with him a part-blood Creek. We will
call the broker "Jim." "Joe Buckskin" was in a small hotel
near by, with one of "Jim's" friends watching so that "Joe"
would not wander away. Chandler and I accompanied "Jim"
to meet "Joe" at the latter's hotel. "Jim" had a lease form
ready to fill out in the name of the company to which the lease
would be made.

The deal had to be made at once, we were told, because
another company was anxiously waiting to sign if we didn't.
(Old stuff, started at the time of the Drake well.) We were
assured that we had the first chance because of the broker's
great admiration for Harry and his regard for me.

We demanded proof that the Indian was "Joe Buckskin."
Many papers were produced for our benefit, but none convinced Ed or me that they were genuine. We asked for a couple
of hours' delay, which was given, but not graciously.

Ed and I then went to the Indian agent's office. Dana H.
Kelsey was the agent. I had never met Kelsey, but understood
that he was a live wire and knew his lines. We explained our
case to him and said that we wanted to bring "Joe" to Kelsey's
office to have him identified.

"I have been trying to get 'Joe' in here for several years,"
said Kelsey. "If you can bring him in I will feel that I should
give you not only my thanks but at least a box of cigars."
Kelsey was of the same opinion that we were, that a ringer
was being used.

On returning to "Jim's" hotel, we told him that we had the

whole matter taken care of, that we all would go to Kelsey's office and on Kelsey's endorsement of "Joe" we would make the contemplated trade. Our proposition was promptly rejected. It was explained that "Joe" was afraid Kelsey might put him in jail for something the Indian had done in the past. "Jim" also had many other reasons why "Joe" should not go to Kelsey's office.

Ed and I packed our bags and returned to Independence with the twenty thousand dollars intact.

5

AN OIL EMPIRE RISES

THE OIL BUSINESS was moving at an accelerated pace from Kansas to Oklahoma—production, pipe-line capacity, and (more gradually) refining. Tulsa was becoming, as it later proudly proclaimed, the "Oil Capital of the World." Its total population in 1912 could not have exceeded twenty-five thousand, but there was no denying its destiny.

Harry Sinclair's holdings in Oklahoma had become many times more valuable than those he had assembled in Kansas. Glenn Pool was by now in full swing. Sinclair was interested in many leases there, and he was pushing an extensive drilling campaign. I was spending most of my time in Tulsa, at Glenn Pool, and on other Sinclair leases. In September, 1912, my family moved to Tulsa, and I purchased a residence at 1407 South Carson.

Sinclair's first offices in Tulsa were at Third and Main streets. Later we moved into the Palace Building at Fourth and Main. In 1918 we moved from there to the eight-story Sinclair Building at Fifth and Main. But our business soon outgrew these quarters and we overflowed into offices in three other buildings. Now, a scant thirty-five years later, we have just completed and occupied a building at Boston Avenue and Tenth Street large enough to accommodate all our office force and still permit expansion in the future.

I had watched Tulsa rise from a village. It was too insignificant to find a place in any standard atlas published at the turn of the century. But by the time of our removal there, it already had acquired some of the basic grace and attractiveness which have since made it one of the fairest cities in the land. Angie Debo has told the story well in *Tulsa: From Creek Town to Oil Capital,* and I need not repeat it here. It had been a Creek Indian place, Lochapoka Tulsey, in the nineteenth century; then a small trading center; and, finally, with the coming of oil after 1905, a swiftly growing, progressive young city straddling the Arkansas River. Only Muskogee sixty miles southeast rivaled it.

There were two landmarks across the Arkansas from the city proper—in West Tulsa—the Constantine Refinery east of the highway leading to Sapulpa about twenty miles away, and the Cosden Oil and Gas Company Refinery on the East side of the highway. They were the beginnings of refinery operations in the area, and were to become very large in later years.

Many independent oil operators were then located in Tulsa: R. A. Josey, Charles Page, Sinclair and White, Gunsberg and Foreman, and Jack Crosby, all of whom were producers, and many others. During the period, most of the oil in Oklahoma and the Southwest was handled by independents rather than by large integrated companies. As a matter of fact, integration was a relatively new principle, even among the so-called majors, and of the latter, the Standard organization was obviously the pioneer.

The coming of the great war in Europe in August, 1914, was not slow in making itself felt, demand-wise, in the oil industry. Almost immediately the Sinclair organization got the impact of increased demand. We were then occupied principally with production and had no refinery installations. But we had a market for every barrel of oil that we took out of the ground from shortly after hostilities started until well after the war closed. By late 1915 we were producing in Oklahoma, Kansas, Texas, Arkansas, and Louisiana. We continued to expand our producing areas during the war, so that by 1919 we were even producing in Wyoming.

It must be understood that, while the armies of Europe were not yet mechanized as they were to become at a subsequent date, nevertheless the requirements of both military and domestic consumption of oil were moving into their modern phase—a phase which possibly would not have arrived as fast had the war not occurred.

Our large and constantly growing oil production was going into essential lubricants, gasoline, and other fuels and lubricating products. Gasoline at that time was principally a fraction made in the refining of crude petroleum, a method quite different from that now employed in the production of motor fuels. But a certain amount of casing-head gasoline (that is, gasoline made from natural gas) was even at that time being produced. As I recall it, there was only one premium grade, and it, like all the rest, was white gasoline.

By this time I had become a stockholder in most of the companies that we were operating. I was also interested, with E. E. Byers, in some cable drilling tools. Cushing, with its flood of oil, was at its crest in the period from 1913 to 1915, and we were drilling a great many wells. We were building steel storage tanks of 55,000 barrels capacity at the same time to take care of the oil produced. Oil was going into some of them before the roofs were finished.

The whole organization, including Harry Sinclair himself, was working about eighteen hours a day, usually seven days a week. Harry F. and Earl W. Sinclair, P. J. White, and his

brother Thomas White were the principal stockholders in
these companies, with F. B. Ufer holding stock in some of
them. I took the leases on many properties, drilled them, and
they were even sold without Harry Sinclair's ever being in on
them. Sinclair was the kind of man who, if he thought you
knew your business, gave you a free hand. If you didn't know
your business, you didn't stay with him.

Many of our leases were sold to the Prairie Oil and Gas
Company, but most if not all of them were to come back to
the Sinclair Company in the merger effected with Prairie in
1932. Harry was a far-sighted builder and a shrewd seller.
And sometimes I think it is even better to know when to sell
than when to buy. In this connection it may be pointed out to
future analysts of the oil industry that finance capital was
slower in coming to the oil country than the sheer logic of
developments would indicate might have been the case. The
pattern of leasing, getting oil production on a small investment, thereby "proving up" the property and perhaps a whole
area, and then selling the producing lease and part or all of the
blocked-up country around it was general in the early years of
this century. This is how we got ready cash for similar or even
larger enterprises. The tempo and thrusting and probing that
resulted were then essential features of the oil game, particularly in the exploratory and drilling phases.

The oil business has always required large sums of money
as well as raw courage and bottomless energy for its development. It has required its followers to look always to the future.
But in the war years, a lot of oil folks just looked good. Wages
went high, and on Saturday nights the members of drilling
crews came out in wide candy-striped silk shirts costing up to
twenty dollars apiece. This was a kind relief from grinding
toil, very long hours, and certain physical risks that had better
be forgotten than recalled.

The war was not a year old when Harry Sinclair was beginning to think of the forging of a "big" company. The word needs quotation marks because by this time almost everything in the oil business was big. Costs were high but still growing; the sums needed for daily operations were sometimes staggering; and anything that resembled integration (production, refining, and marketing, all joined under one management) called for really great resources.

But late in 1915 differences between Sinclair and Pat and Tom White arose, necessitating the sale in January, 1916, of the producing properties which had formerly been operated by this group. These were very extensive properties, and the sale to produce a division of assets was a complicated affair.

With Frank Haskell, president of the Okla Oil Company, I put in many days and nights inspecting the properties and working over the production and equipment records. After several meetings in Tulsa, Haskell said he liked the properties, and that if a satisfactory price could be arrived at his company would like to acquire them. He asked Sinclair and White to go on to New York and meet with his principals. The Whites left for New York, as did Sinclair and I. After we arrived in New York, Sinclair decided that it would be wise for Edward H. Chandler, general counsel for the Sinclair Oil and Gas Company, to be with us, and accordingly Chandler joined us. We met with Dickson Q. Brown and Robert Mc-Kelvey at the New York offices of the Tidewater Oil Company. The Okla Oil Company was a subsidiary of the Tidewater.

A trade was finally closed, and the Okla Oil Company became owner of the Kathleen Oil Company, the Scioto Oil Company, Only Oil Company, and Oil Production Company, besides some small companies and individual leases.

Sinclair and Chandler remained in New York to draw up a contract between Sinclair and the Whites and the Tidal; also a contract between Sinclair and the Whites whereby Sinclair purchased the Whites' interest in the undrilled acreage owned jointly by them and Sinclair.

On Sinclair's return to Tulsa, he organized the Sinclair Oil Company. The stockholders were H. F. Sinclair, E. W. Sinclair, Edward H. Chandler, W. A. Martin, O. E. Dougherty, Albert E. Watts, and myself. H. F. Sinclair was president, Chandler and I were vice presidents, and E. W. Sinclair was secretary and treasurer. Watts was placed in charge of the land department. I was given charge of the drilling and production. We at once started drilling the acreage purchased from the Whites.

Harry Sinclair now began the realization of his long-cherished dream of building a large, fully integrated oil company.

On November 20, 1915, W. H. Isom, president of the Cudahy Refining Company, in Chicago, wrote to Sinclair the following letter:

November 20, 1915.

Personal & Confidential

Mr. Harry F. Sinclair,
Tulsa, Okla.
My dear Mr. Sinclair:

At different times I have talked with you, you seemed to be more than interested in the refinery and pipe line business, and have expressed a desire to get in the game, and on one deal you proposed, or offered, to take considerable stock in the project with the Cudahys. At that time I told you the Cudahy Refining Co. was a close corporation, and had no outsiders in it, and this, for that matter, is the case at present, but in the final closing up of the Michael Cudahy Estate, it has been necessary to change about many of the corporations connected with the Estate, and among them the Cudahy Refining Co., and in making the change in this Company, there will be $300,000 to $500,000 Capital Stock to place. The plan has been to have different members of the family take over this

58

stock. Now I have had the feeling I wanted some "new blood" with us, and those that could do us some good in the way of securing business, supply of crude oils, etc., and have partially secured consent to let some outsiders have some of this stock, and this made me think of yourself. Will you kindly advise if you are still in the mood to consider an investment of this kind and if so, would you care to take a block of this stock? It goes without saying that it is a profitable investment, and will stand the most rigid investigation.

It is true there has not been much "hurrah" about us and our methods of doing business. We go ahead in our quiet way, but the fact remains, we "get there," and always have. Personally, I should like to have with us a few "live ones" like you are, and this is why I am writing you. It is not money we need, and the stock need not go begging one moment, and offered on the market with the showing we make, would be snapped up quickly, but I want to see it go where it will do us the most good.

With kindest personal regards, I remain

> Yours truly,
> [signed]   W. H. Isom

This was one of those not quite fortuitous situations (Harry Sinclair had already approached the Cudahy interests about a refining connection) in which both sides are not only willing but actually need each other. Sinclair had a lot of production but no refining outlets of his own; the Cudahys had the refinery but were in need of a producing connection to supply it.

Shortly after receipt of the foregoing letter, Sinclair visited Isom at the latter's office in Chicago and discussed with him the idea of making the Cudahy Refining Company a part of the new integrated oil company which Sinclair had in mind. Isom was impressed and said that when Sinclair's idea had been made a reality he would recommend that the Cudahys go along. So the state was set for a refinery to be one of the units in Sinclair's projected company.

Meantime, I had a few chores of my own. After closing a trade for the Ardsworth Oil Company at Ardmore, I started for Tulsa. It was necessary to change trains at Oklahoma City. While I was in a hotel there waiting for train time, Al Watts called me from St. Louis and asked me to be in Pawhuska the next morning, to purchase some of the producing leases that had been drilled by T. N. Barnsdall. The secretary of the interior had declared these leases to be excess acreage beyond the legal limit established for Barnsdall in the Osage Leasing Act, and had ordered them sold.

At the sale the next day, April 21, 1916, I accordingly purchased the following Barnsdall tracts: Lot 54, with 259 barrels production, for $241,355.84; Lot 68, 58 barrels, $46,505; Tract 22, 26 barrels, $31,661; Tract 40, 12 barrels, $4,670; Tract 90, 46 barrels, $71,880; Tract 96, 59 barrels, $51,127: a total of $447,198.84. Since that April day thirty-eight years ago, many of the leases purchased have continued producing and are still owned by the Sinclair Oil and Gas Company. The Prairie Oil and Gas Company also purchased many leases at this sale, and they also are now owned by the Sinclair Oil and Gas Company under the subsequent merger which I have noted.

I reported to Sinclair on the leases that I had purchased at the Pawhuska sale and the amount of money spent. "Good work, Billy," he said. "But you should have spent another $500,000. We will make a lot of money on that deal. Those leases will be producing twenty-five years from now." And so they are, and then some.

While we were purchasing these companies and leases, Sinclair had decided upon the character and structure of his large integrated company. He left for New York, accompanied by Chandler, and organized the Sinclair Oil and Refining Company, with a capital of fifty million dollars.

The meetings in New York were held in the offices of

Spooner, Cotton and Franklin, attorneys. On April 22, 1916, newspapers carried the story of this new giant in the oil world. It was of great interest to the entire oil industry, especially the Midcontinent field. The following article appeared in the *Tulsa World* of April 22, 1916:

GIGANTIC OIL CORPORATION FORMED BY HARRY SINCLAIR
WITH $50,000,000 CAPITAL

WILL BE FOURTH LARGEST IN THE ENTIRE COUNTRY

To Combine Production of Cudahy, Chanute
and Milliken Refineries

DEAL IS COMPLETED

Five Leading New York Banks With Tulsa Man
Behind Enterprise

(By J. A. M'Keever)

Formation of a gigantic oil corporation for the purpose of producing, refining and marketing crude oil and its products was announced here yesterday by H. F. Sinclair, wealthy oil producer and former baseball magnate on his return from New York City, where he had been for several weeks. The new company, which will be headed by Mr. Sinclair, has a capital stock of $50,000,000 and will be known as the Sinclair Oil and Refining Company. Mr. Sinclair is president of the corporation.

With physical assets of over $55,000,000 this company takes its position as one of the four largest oil corporations in the United States. The new company will combine the production of the Sinclair Oil Company and possibly other well known producing firms with the production, pipe lines and plants of three of the largest independent refining companies in the west, according to reports, which, while not authorized by the organizer, are undoubtedly true. The three refining companies which have gone into the new combination are the Cudahy, Chanute and Milliken refining companies. The physical properties of the new corporation to start with will have, at a very conservative calculation, a value of $55,000,000. The new company will be the largest strictly independent oil concern in this country.

Mr. Sinclair returned to Tulsa at noon yesterday from New York, where he has been successful in organizing the new company and placing its securities, and stated that five of the largest banks in New York were behind the proposition. He declined at this time to give the names of the banks in the deal.

"I have been studying this proposition for a long time," said Mr. Sinclair, "and I believe the time is ripe for just the kind of an organization we intend this to be. The combining of the producing, refining and marketing ends of the oil industry under one management gives the ideal method of 'playing the game.' "

"Never before in the history of the oil industry," continued Mr. Sinclair, "did conditions look so bright as they do now. The new automobiles to be put into service this year alone will receive the entire gasoline output of sixty thousand barrels of crude petroleum per day, to say nothing of the vast amount of new tractors, gasoline engines, etc., that are being built and the automobiles already in service. This new company will have ample financial backing to go into most any kind of a proposition. I want to deny the report that it is organized to compete with the Standard Oil Company. We expect to produce oil, to refine it and to sell it in the markets of this country and the world in competition with anybody."

WON'T DIVULGE DETAILS

Mr. Sinclair declined to give out additional details as to the plans of the new company beyond admitting that incorporation papers would be taken out in New York on the 27th of the present month, giving the organization a great latitude in conducting its varied lines of business.

However, from very good authority it can be stated that the new company plans to build a pipe line to the east, where more than likely a large refinery will be built in addition to the plants now in operation, to take care of demands for refined products in territory not reached by the refineries to be taken over by the new corporation.

The Sinclair Oil Company which Mr. Sinclair heads since the dissolution and sale of the producing properties of the famous partnership of White and Sinclair, a few months ago, has been rapidly acquiring production in Oklahoma and today has about 7,000 barrels per day with options on other properties. This production combined with the production owned by the refineries and others interested in the new company give the Sinclair Oil and Refining Company a daily production of over 14,000 barrels a day to start with.

MILES OF PIPE LINES

Several hundred miles of pipe lines owned by the three refineries go into the deal. The Cudahy Company has 112 miles of pipe line, the Chanute refinery 128 miles and the Milliken Company 121 miles in Kansas and Oklahoma.

The three refining companies together own five refining plants with a total daily refining capacity at the present time of 16,000 barrels of oil per day. These capacities can be easily increased and all the plants are strictly modern with improved processes for extracting more gasoline.

Several smaller tracts in other fields were purchased and Thursday W. L. Connelly bid in several hundred barrels of production at the Osage sale. These properties and others which are under consideration will give the Sinclair Oil and Refining Company a big start in the production end.

The Milliken Oil Company, subsidiary of the Milliken Refining Company, owns a half interest in the Minnehoma Oil Company property at Cushing which has a daily production of six hundred barrels. 112 miles of main lines owned by the Cudahy Company and the Milliken Refining Company has a total of 121 miles making a total of 361 miles of main lines owned by the new concern in Kansas and Oklahoma.

IMPORTANT FACTOR

The size of the new interests, together with the fact that it will be an important factor in the oil history of this country, leads to the belief that a pipe line to eastern seaboards is only the matter of a short time.

The size of the refineries purchased by the Sinclair company compare favorably with any in this part of the country. The Milliken refinery, located at Vinita, Okla., was built in 1910, at a cost of $1,000,000, but since that time a wax plant has been added and other improvements added, which will bring the value of the plant to over $2,000,000. This plant has a capacity of six thousand barrels daily and this plant has also expended over $35,000 on the Snelling process for extracting more gasoline from oil than is possible with the accepted methods.

TAKES OVER CHANUTE

The Chanute Refining Company, another concern taken over by the new company, has two plants, one of two thousand barrel capacity, located at Chanute, Kan., and the other, a most modern affair, with a capacity of four thousand barrels, located at Cushing, Okla.

These plants were built in 1914 and cost $300,000, but additions to both plants put the combined value up to nearly one and one-half million dollars.

The Cudahy Refining Company has a large plant at Coffeyville, Kan., built in 1908, at a cost of $1,000,000, and a small plant built in 1905, at a cost of $95,000. The capacity of the plants are three thousand and three hundred barrels respectively.

The other refining companies included in the merger all have some production, and the Chanute people are drilling several wild-cat tests. The Sinclair Oil Company has thousands of acres of leases, several hundred acres of which look mighty good now.

Harry Ford Sinclair, who has organized and who will be the president and active head of the company, has had a meteoric career in the oil industry since his entry, about seven years ago. Several times he has built up fine producing properties and sold out at a big profit each time, his last sale coming a few months ago when he and his recent partner, P. J. White, realized close to $10,000,000 from their production.

BASEBALL MAGNATE

Two years ago he appeared on the baseball horizon as one of the principal factors in the baseball fight between organized ball and the Federal League. As one of the big backers of the Federal League he became a power in baseball, as well as in oil circles, and was largely instrumental in bringing about peace. In return for the money he put into the new league, Sinclair was given the right to dispose of many Federal League stars, which he did at a big price.

Although no statement was to be had as to where the general offices of the new company would be located, it was intimated they would be in Tulsa, which will largely add to the prestige of this city as the leading oil center of the world.

The officers of the new corporation were: H. F. Sinclair, president; Joseph M. Cudahy and W. H. Isom, vice presidents; E. W. Sinclair, secretary and treasurer; E. B. Huston, assistant secretary and treasurer; A. E. Watts, assistant to the president. The directors were: H. F. Sinclair, E. W. Sinclair, W. H. Isom, Joseph M. Cudahy, O. M. Gerstung, E. B. Huston, William Hutteg, E. R. Kemp, J. W. Perry, W. L. Connelly, G. W. Davidson, J. Fletcher Farrell, Samuel L. Fuller, H. B. McCune, J. R. Manion, Ray Morris, Acosta Nichols, Theodore Roosevelt, Jr., H. P. Wright, and Albert Strauss.

The following subsidiary companies were organized to handle producing, pipe-line, and refining activities:

Sinclair Refining Company: W. H. Isom, president; Joseph M. Cudahy and C. A. Bradley, vice presidents; J. R. Murray, secretary; J. Fletcher Farrell, treasurer; D. S. Parmelee, assistant secretary and treasurer.

Sinclair Oil and Gas Company: H. F. Sinclair, president; Joseph M. Cudahy and E. R. Kemp, vice presidents; E. W.

Sinclair, secretary and treasurer; E. B. Huston, assistant secretary and treasurer.

Sinclair-Cudahy Pipe Line Company: Joseph M. Cudahy, president; H. F. Sinclair and W. L. Connelly, vice presidents; E. W. Sinclair, secretary and treasurer; E. B. Huston, assistant secretary and treasurer; John R. Manion, general manager.

All of the properties of the Sinclair Oil Company developed or purchased prior to or during the organization of the Sinclair Oil & Refining Corporation were transferred to the respective companies handling production, pipe lines, and refineries of that corporation.

Through these consolidations and new companies we acquired all of the properties previously described and new production at Garber, Oklahoma, and through the Milliken Oil and Refining Company we acquired the Slick Oil Company, the Katy Oil Company, and a one-half interest in the Leta Kolvin Lease at Drumright. The title to the Kolvin Lease was to become the subject of litigation extending over thirty years. Within the last three years the dispute was finally settled in Sinclair's favor. The price paid for the Milliken Oil and Refining Company, $10,000,000, was at that time the highest ever paid in Oklahoma for an oil company.

In addition to these properties the following companies and their producing properties had been purchased: Healdton Oil and Gas Company, Ardsworth Oil Company, Toxoway Oil Company, Beaver Oil Company, and Ufer and Galbreath. Some smaller properties were also purchased.

The New York offices of the Sinclair interests, in the Equitable Building, 120 Broadway, were rented from Charles J. Wrightsman, our old friend of the Chaser Oil Company adventure. All branches of the corporation were busy. My activities were almost entirely confined to the pipe line company, with occasional outside assignments. One of these was

Zaxamixtle (Golden Lane, south of Tampico, State of Vera Cruz, Mexico), about 1918. Two wells on fire, one of 20,000 and one of 40,000 barrels per day.

W. L. Connelly, A. E. Watts, and O. E. Dougherty, on
Teapot Dome, December, 1922—the winters were cold.

the purchase of the Adams-Linn Farm in Butler County, Kansas. Again a trade with Charley Wrightsman.

On another mission I made a trip to Wyoming to look over some lands owned by the Cudahy family. I went first from Tulsa to Lander, Wyoming. After inspecting the Cudahy holdings, I drove to Lost Soldier, where a well was being drilled with a small Star drilling machine. This well was completed in June, 1916, in the First Wall Creek sand, coming in for about two hundred barrels of oil at a total depth of 269 feet. I little thought that sixteen years later these Lost Soldier leases were to be part of the properties in the merger between the Sinclair and Prairie companies. From many different sands they have produced millions of barrels of oil, and they will produce many more millions.

Sinclair had no pipe-line organization. We reached into the Prairie Pipe Line Company and engaged the services of John R. Manion as general manager; Frank Hadley, chief engineer; Jim Blake, general superintendent. From the Texas Company we took J. W. (Jack) Jordan, who was made chief gauger. Many other pipe-liners were hired away from other pipe-line companies, and an organization was quickly formed. Jack Jordan went into the army in World War I, and after his discharge I put him in charge of properties at Damon Mound, Texas. When Jim Flanagan wanted a superintendent in Louisiana, Jack went to Homer. From there he went with me to Wyoming, then to a vice presidency, and finally to the executive vice presidency.

A refinery was to be built at East Chicago, Illinois. We had to build a pipe line from Drumright to East Chicago to supply oil to it; also many field and gathering lines. The East Chicago line was for months in 1916 and 1917 the cause of many headaches in the entire organization. It was a day-and-night job. Manion and I spent almost all of our nights on sleepers. During the day we purchased pipe, pumps, engines, and the hundred and one other needed requirements. The right-of-way across Illinois posed a terrific problem, but finally the line was completed, and oil was being pumped into the refinery which had meantime been completed.

The building of this line was the subject of much sport among some of the larger companies. It was declared that we should have built our refinery in central Illinois, that we never would get into East Chicago with a pipe line. Again Sinclair showed up his critics. Manion and Blake deserve much credit for the successful completion of the line. So also do the right-of-way men, who fought their way under tremendous difficulties. But with H. F. urging us on, there was never a thought of failure.

Aside from being one of the largest Midcontinent producers of oil, Sinclair, after the formation of the integrated company in 1916, swiftly became one of the largest purchasers of crude oil as well. The added quantities of oil were needed to supplement our own production in supplying our newly acquired refinery and pipe-line properties. For the purposes of purchasing crude, we had organized the Sinclair Crude Oil Purchasing Company.

We as a nation were now only months away from involvement in World War I. The pressure for oil in all its forms increased from week to week. This meant, among other things, that refiners had to buy steadily, and, when necessary, set the pace in buying. On December 20, 1916, the Sinclair Oil and Gas Company advanced the price of Midcontinent oil to $1.30 a barrel, an increase of 10 cents over the prevailing price. This was the third time since the Midcontinent field had been opened that the price on the local market had been changed by any company other than the Prairie Oil and Gas Company.

In the meantime, our refineries, under the direction of W. H. Isom, had been functioning to their capacity. Berry

Griffith came into the oil company as a vice president at this time. He later was elected to the presidency.

The company had been operating for over a year, and we officials began to have some leisure. I had taken up golf, but was, and remained, only a dub at it. One afternoon in July, 1917, Jim Flanagan, John Harrington, and I decided to play a round. The Tulsa Country Club, as I remember, had the only golf course in Tulsa. We were members, so there was where we were to play. The membership of the club was made up of oilmen, bankers, and businessmen. I can remember seeing men like Dr. W. A. Cook, T. K. Smith, Tom Chestnut, Henry N. Greis, A. E. Bradshaw, John H. Markham, Jr., Ernest Connelly, Doug Franchott, S. G. Kennedy, Roger Kemp and Frank Moore among those who played there.

We joked and chaffed each other as we drove out to the club that day. We had shoved aside work and we welcomed the relaxation and companionship in prospect. There was the usual good-natured banter as we teed off.

A few dark clouds appeared while we were playing the first seven holes, boding nothing more serious than a possible shower. We were about to drive from the No. 8 tee when a rainstorm blew up. We decided to play the hole anyway.

Flanagan and Harrington both drove ahead of me (everybody always did). I sliced my drive and had trouble finding the ball. The two others played on and were a shot ahead of me. Both were on the green, and I was about twenty-five feet away when a flaming bolt of lightning crashed.

I was stunned momentarily. When my mind began to function again, I realized that I was holding my head with both hands. My caddy, Orville Sinclair, was standing near me, crying. I noted a red streak on one of his forearms. "Mr. Flanagan is calling you," he managed to say.

I looked about and saw Jim circling aimlessly some thirty feet from the green and holding a handkerchief to his mouth.

69

I tried to go to him, but had difficulty in controlling my legs.

"What's the matter, Jim?" I asked when I eventually reached him.

"I'm all right," he gasped, "but look at John—he's dead!"

There lay John, face down, on the green, with his head over the cup. We turned him over. There was no sign of life.

"A pulmotor!" exclaimed Jim, and he started for the clubhouse to telephone for one.

One of the caddies had already started to summon help. The two others stayed with me.

Another cracking flash of lightning split the sky. It sent a shiver along my spine, but caused no further damage. The caddies and I then started for the clubhouse. Meantime R. D. Stauffer and Police Commissioner Al Funk, who had been in the clubhouse, got into a car and started driving across the links to the No. 8 green. Al said I fell down twice in the short distance I had covered before the two reached me. Stauffer got me into the car and took me to the clubhouse. Funk went to where Harrington lay.

Jim had got in touch with the Tulsa Fire Department, and a few minutes later a squad of firemen, with a pulmotor, arrived. But John was beyond resuscitation. The lightning bolt had killed him instantly. He was buried at Wellsville, New York, his birthplace.

My ears were affected by the shock I had experienced, and for several days I was partly deaf.

6

BUSINESS, BULLETS,
ANTS IN THE PANTS

EARLY IN 1917 Harry F. Sinclair made a trade with E. M. Sims, of Houston, Texas, by which he acquired the Freeport and Tampico Oil Corporation. This corporation owned as subsidiaries the Freeport Mexican Fuel Oil Company and the Freeport Mexican Transportation Company, as well as a refinery at Mereaux, Louisiana, later. The name of the Freeport Mexican Fuel Oil Company was later changed to Mexican Sinclair Oil Corporation, and I was then elected president.

The Freeport Mexican Transportation Company owned two tankers, the *Panuco* and the *Tamesi,* each of about thirty thousand barrels carrying capacity. It also owned two Ohio River tank steamers, which hauled barges loaded with oil from Panuco on the Panuco River to a small terminal at Tampico, near the Gulf of Mexico. There this oil was transferred to the tankers, some to be taken to Mereaux, where it was refined, and the rest to Galveston, Texas, where it was sold as fuel oil. The *Panuco* and the *Tamesi* were the start of the magnificent fleet of tankers now owned by the Sinclair Oil Corporation.

At the time of these purchases from Sims, I was moved to Houston from which point I was to supervise Mexico opera-

71

tions. Al Watts was made president of the three companies, and I vice president. The Sinclair Refining Company now began construction of the Houston refinery on the ship channel. I was made a vice president of this company. In addition to the posts named, I was elected a director of the Union National Bank, Houston, and I served in that capacity during the remainder of my residence in the city. The manifold responsibilities I had accepted kept me busy.

James P. Flanagan, of Tulsa, was elected treasurer of these various Sinclair units and sent to Houston. When the Sinclair Oil and Gas Company of Louisiana established its main office in Shreveport, he moved to that city as president of the corporation. He was succeeded as treasurer in Houston by John W. Stanford of Independence, Kansas.

It was necessary for me to make many trips to Tampico. Most of them were made to our tankers. Some were made by rail, but Mexico was in such a turbulent state that rail travel was slow and dangerous. Friendly relations prevailed among oil companies operating in Mexico and owning tankers, and it was not unusual for me to ride to and from Tampico on ships other than our own.

In November, 1917, I made my first trip to Mexico. Al Watts, John Manion, N.G.M. Luykx, and some others were in the party. The trip was made by train through Laredo, Texas, to Tampico. It was a dilly. No Pullmans, no diners. Manion and I came back on a Standard Oil Company tanker, the *Charles D. Pratt,* and had a pleasant time. Watts and the others drove back to Laredo by auto—a nightmare trip. Manion and I spent a week or more in Mexico visiting the properties and arranging for future work.

Dan Moran, then vice president in charge of affairs for the Texas Company in Mexico, had a nice house in the foreign colony district of Tampico, and I spent many of my nights with him while in that city.

72

Henry W. Sharp was our resident manager, with an office in Tampico, and Walter Tschudin was assistant manager. Oil produced from the wells at Panuco, as I have previously indicated, was taken down the Panuco River in wooden barges pushed by stern-wheel steamers of the Ohio River type and pumped into tankers for delivery at Houston and at Havana and other ports in Cuba, as well as to our refinery at Mereaux, Louisiana. It was a slow and costly procedure, as the Panuco River was full of turns and twists. We later built a pump station on the Zurita lease, put in eleven miles of pipe line, and delivered oil to barges below most of the curves. This pipe line eliminated thirty-two miles of river hauling. In addition we built near the entrance of the Panuco into the Gulf of Mexico a large terminal and tank farm, also large docks, where we could load two tankers at one time.

Our operations were extended to the southern field, particularly to the Golden Lane, a narrow oil belt between Tampico and Tuxpan. The largest well that I remember our drilling was No. 1, Lot 114 Chinampa. As I remember, this well produced sixty thousand to seventy thousand barrels daily. None of the wells lasted long, because we produced them to their full capacity and naturally they drew in salt water fast. This No. 1 Chinampa was the first well in Mexico, to my knowledge, to be produced under back pressure, which, simply stated, is the controlled application of natural gas pressure in the sand to the natural lifting or flow of oil up the well.

On one of my visits to the Golden Lane I stopped at this well. It had been shut in for several months. I wondered if the well would again produce oil if the valves were opened only a little; in other words, if the valves were "cracked." We decided to try out this theory. After several days' production of salt water only, the well started to produce oil. In the meantime the Atlantic Refining Company, which had been running the oil to its station about four miles distant, had taken out its eight-inch pipe line. After several conferences we induced the company to replace its line, and we produced about one thousand barrels of oil daily from this well for quite a long period. As I remember, we sold the oil at 51 cents a barrel at the well.

The Zurita lease at Panuco had a wonderful recovery. No. 3 well must have produced about 20,000,000 barrels of oil during its life. This was a heavy black oil, 11.2 degrees.

Revolutions were almost always on tap in Mexico at that time, and we were continually in trouble with one or another of the many self-appointed leaders.

During one of my visits to Mexico we took a trip in a company-owned launch, the *Claro,* to view some leases that had been offered to us. Accompanying me were Walter Tschudin, assistant manager of Sinclair operations in Mexico; Grover Clark, W. T. Lestergette, two Mexican boatmen, and Wan Wang, a Chinese cook. The leases were up the Tamesi River. The launch had good eating and sleeping accommodations and was quite comfortable in general.

On the return trip we decided to put in to shore, catch some fish, and have our dinner, then proceed to Tampico. Just as we were about to give the order to the boatmen there was an explosion, and the forward part of the boat burst into flames. The two boatmen were caught in the fire and both jumped overboard, swimming to shore. The Chinese cook, who could not swim, also leaped into the water. Clark made an effort to save him but failed, and Wan Wang drowned. Tschudin and Lestergette tied a rope to the rail of the boat at the stern and swam to the shore, taking with them the other end of the rope, which they tied to a tree. I went hand-over-hand on this rope to the shore.

There was a small native house near where we landed. Clark and Lestergette secured a boat, made grappling-hooks, and rowed to the spot where Wan Wang had sunk. They recovered his body. Late that night a native boat came down the river. We hailed it and were taken aboard and on to Tampico. We put the cook's body in a small boat and towed it with us. The launch meantime had burned to the water's edge and sunk.

We were a sorry-looking outfit when we arrived at Tampico. We had used our shirts to make bandages for one of the Mexican boatmen, who had been badly burned. We had lost our boots, and I had lost my glasses.

Another time, Tschudin and I went to Tampico from the lower country. We were in a fast launch belonging to the company. While we were going through the Chihole Canal, bandits on the shore started shooting at us. Walter and I at once lay down in the bottom of the boat. Antonio, our boatman, sat at his post, opened the engine to its top speed, and ran us through the fusillade without anyone's being hurt.

I had been told that these Mexican outlaws were notoriously poor marksmen, and our experience tended to substantiate this view. Nevertheless, the emotion stirred by those whistling bullets was something less than pure delight.

While well No. 1 on Lot 114 Chinampa was being drilled, we had our camp about three-quarters of a mile south of the well site. We walked between the camp and the well on the narrow-gauge railroad which had been built to transport oil-field supplies. After spending a night at the camp, Tschudin and I rose early one morning to walk to the well, which was about ready for completion.

He had gone a short distance when Walter began slapping his legs, jumping, and dancing about in a most undignified fashion. I watched his antics in amazement. Although a good-natured fellow, Walter had never shown any disposition to play the clown. Besides that, the expression on his face indicated clearly he was far from being in a frolicsome mood. He never had shown the smallest sign of mental derangement, but what could be wrong? To my urgent demand, "What's the matter, Walter?" he made no reply.

After several minutes of this arresting acrobatic performance, Walter started on a dead run for the camp, emitting wild yelps and strange, blood-freezing maledictions. I followed him back to the camp, where I ascertained the cause of his highly original show. During the night, while he slept, an army of ants had crawled into his trousers and camped there. They gave no evidence of their presence until he began to move briskly about. Then they gave plenty. "Ants in the pants" was something more than a figure of speech.

The next year, in 1918, the American Oil Producers in Mexico engaged the services of James R. Garfield, former Secretary of the Interior, and Nelson Rhodes, a Los Angeles attorney, to appear before the Mexican government for consideration of a proposed amendment to the Mexican constitution. Garfield, a member of the Cleveland law firm of Garfield, Garfield and Howe, was a son of the martyred president. The amendment under discussion affected the interests of Americans with oil holdings in Mexico.

Al Watts was selected to go to Mexico City with these men to counsel with them on matters as they developed. Watts asked Henry Sharp, our manager in Mexico, and me to accompany him on the mission. We spent several weeks in the conferences that followed. During our stay there we made many new acquaintances, among them Jules Bertheir, a mining man.

Bertheir one day invited Watts, Sharp, Garfield, Rhodes, Van Trees, an export agent, Carl H. Smith, a banker, and me for dinner at his home. It was arranged that Van should call at the hotel to accompany Watts, Sharp, and me to Bertheir's. Sharp was indisposed and unable to go with us. Before we left the hotel Van asked me how much money I had with me. "A couple of hundred dollars," I replied.

"That's not enough," Van responded, with a shake of his head. "We're going to play poker after dinner."

"Who's been talking to you about my poker playing and giving you the idea that two hundred dollars isn't enough for an evening?" I asked.

"No one," he returned, "but we undoubtedly will play a stiff game."

Thus forewarned, I went to Sharp's room and borrowed six hundred dollars from him. I felt sure I wouldn't lose that much, regardless of how stiff the game might be. Watts, equally desirous of being prepared for whatever eventualities the game might hold, went across the street to the Sanborn Restaurant and cashed some traveler's checks.

Following the dinner, Garfield and Rhodes, having some business to attend to, left. We then went to Bertheir's gun room. A card table had been set up there, with chips at the five chairs placed around it. Under each stack of chips was a slip of paper marked "2250." Interpreting this as meaning $2,250, I made a quick resolution to play cautiously, for sterner competition than I was accustomed to seemed to be in prospect.

Watts is a worse player than I am. (Ask H.F.S.) Getting him aside, I advised in an undertone, "Play 'em close; I'll do the same." And we exchanged glances which meant that if we were headed for defeat we at least would go down fighting.

As we were about to begin playing, Bertheir handed Smith a folded sheet of paper, remarking as he did so, "Carl, I'd like to have you read this aloud when we finish the game. I'm sure it will be of interest to our friends from New York." His action stirred a moment's curiosity in my mind, and then was forgotten in the excitement of the game.

We played till about midnight. Luck had been gracious to both Watts and me. Imposing stacks of blue chips stood in front of us. A rough calculation indicated that our combined winnings were in the neighborhood of four thousand dollars. We were about to cash in when Bertheir said casually, "Well, Carl, it's time to read our letter now."

The "letter" revealed that the game to which Watts and I had devoted our utmost craft and strategy was the kind regularly played by Bertheir and his friends and that the chips stacked in front of us at the start had represented, not $2,250, but 22.50 pesos, or about $11.25 in United States currency.

There was a moment of silence as Watts and I awoke to the fact that we were victims of a practical joke, then laughter, in which all joined. Any chagrin which Watts and I felt was not produced by the sudden deflation of our evening's loot, but by the realization that we had been taken in so guilelessly by those three conspiring pranksters.

Mrs. Bertheir entered the room at this juncture. She was returning from a Red Cross meeting, for this was during World War I. Watts and I handed our "four thousand dollars" to her for the Red Cross.

7

THE CEASELESS QUEST

By the time the war had closed in November, 1918, the Sinclair Oil and Refining Company, parent of all our companies and the center of their integration, had expanded greatly in all of its operations—production, pipe lines, refining, and sales. We had established the Sinclair name widely in the marketing of fuels and lubricants. We were now well established also as purchasers and refiners, as well as producers.

All through the war, the motor car and truck manufacturing industries had been growing. Now, as peace returned, the nation and the world were to see an enormous expansion of these industries, the construction of thousands of miles of public highways, paved streets, and all of the other appurtenances necessary to fast transportation by motor car, bus, and airplane. For the war had not only provided the impetus for the extension of family transportation to America's millions, but had taken the airplane out of the curiosity stage and made it a potential of tremendous importance to our future. All of these developments were to have a profound effect upon the oil industry in general, and upon the Sinclair companies in particular.

By well-planned purchases and extensions, the Sinclair companies were to achieve in 1919 and after an excellent distributing organization. In June, 1919, for example, Harry Sinclair purchased the controlling interest in the Union Oil Company of Philadelphia. This company had many filling stations, which gave us outlets for gasoline and refined products. During these years also the refining company had been erecting filling stations in various locations. The refinery on the ship channel at Houston had been completed, also a refinery at Kansas City, Kansas. To these extensive refining and marketing facilities was added the Pierce Oil Corporation a decade later, by purchase in June, 1930. This company had a good refinery at Tampico, Mexico, and filling stations in many cities of Mexico. It also had a small refinery at Sand Springs, Oklahoma, which we acquired at the time of purchase.

The New York office had meantime been moved from 120 Broadway to the Liberty Tower Building, 45 Nassau Street. The corporation purchased the building in February, 1921, where it remained until it moved to 630 Fifth Avenue, New York. Here it retained offices until July, 1951, when it moved to the Sinclair Oil Building at 600 Fifth Avenue, New York.

Soon after the Sinclair Oil and Refining Company came into existence, other oil companies were organized. Some of these grew into huge corporations. Some fell by the way or were merged with others. Among the signally successful ventures was the Skelly Oil Company, which, under the leadership of W. G. (Bill) Skelly, has had a remarkable growth.

Bill Skelly was and is a real oilman. He learned the business the hard way. He was a tool-dresser, a driller, and did all the work that must be done on an oil lease. He is the only man in Tulsa who was at the head of a large oil company thirty years ago and still holds the same position. The heads of all the other large companies have been changed many times.

80

Bill has surrounded himself with able lieutenants, including C. C. Herndon, Al Cashman, J. A. Freeman, and others of like ability.

Warren Petroleum Corporation is another of the successful producing companies. It was organized in March, 1922, with $300,000 capital, and from an humble start has grown to a corporation with a capital and surplus of $50,000,000. Bill Warren is an able executive with plenty of vision. With the assistance of Joe LaFortune, Howard Felt, Jack Padon, Jim Allison, Don Connelly, Ed Calvert, Sam Hulse, Bill Hartz, and others, he has built one of the outstanding companies in the Midcontinent.

E. W. Marland, like many another in his time, started out with a great head of steam for large accomplishments. His progress was more by spurts than steady, as John Joseph Mathews has shown in his excellent biography of Marland entitled *Life and Death of an Oilman*. His ambition was for a great integrated company, but he fell upon hard times, borrowed heavily, and in the end lost control of the Marland Oil Company, which was absorbed by Continental as the Great Depression began. In his subsequent political career, as a representative in Congress from Oklahoma and as governor of the state, he proved himself capable of constructive thinking, even of an imaginative grasp of many of the problems of his time. But he seemed to have lost some of the great resolution of his youth, and at the close of his governorship, he retired to private life and died shortly thereafter.

J. S. (Josh) Cosden, a colorful character, organized the Cosden Oil and Gas Corporation and operated the Cosden Refinery in West Tulsa, now controlled by the Mid-Continent Petroleum Corporation, which in recent years has attained a capacity of 45,000 barrels per day. This large and efficient oil company is headed by R. W. McDowell as president.

Phillips Petroleum Company was incorporated in 1917 by Frank and L. E. Phillips. Frank was president of the company from its incorporation until April, 1938, when he was elected chairman of the board of directors. This title he retained until his death on August 23, 1950. In April, 1938, K. S. (Boots) Adams was elected president. Adams was made chairman of the board on April 24, 1951, and Paul Endacott succeeded him as president on the same date.

This company has grown from a modest little enterprise to one of the large integrated oil companies. Much of the credit can be attributed to the leadership of Frank Phillips. Frank was a clever businessman and an oil executive who believed in research, which has richly paid off in his company. During the last few years of Frank's life he paid little attention to details, leaving most of them for Boots to handle, and the job was well done. While I am not so well acquainted with Mr. Endacott, I know him for an able successor to the company's splendid former heads. In Charles P. Dimit, vice president in charge of production, the Phillips Petroleum Company has, in my opinion, one of the best men in the producing part of the business.

Henry L. Doherty was the organizer and the man behind the gun for Cities Service Company. He built it into one of the great integrated organizations of American oil. Doherty was, I believe, the first man to advocate the unitization of leases. The idea was slow to be adopted, but is now an accepted practice in the industry. In fact, nearly all companies are strongly in favor of it, and many units are now formed each year. Because it is one of the great advances in the field of conservation, I should describe it for the reader's information as well as for the record of Henry L. Doherty.

Unitization is the oil industry's own interpretation of the law of the conservation of energy. It works like this: if five companies have adjoining leases in an unproven area, they

Teapot Dome—39 miles north of Casper.

Well No. 14, SW ¼ 2–38–78, Teapot Dome, flowing at a rate of 2,000 barrels per hour, 41 gravity oil, through 12½-inch casing from a depth of only 1,515 feet in shale. Drilled October 5, 1922.

Standard (wooden) drilling rig
used in the early 1920's.

Large gas well on Teapot Dome
being closed in (W. L. Connelly far
right; Jack Jordan closing valve).

Steam drilling boiler of the type
used in the early 1920's with standard drilling tools (cable), fueled
from gas on location, or oil, coal,
or wood.

may join together and drill one well, instead of seperate wells upon five properties. A necessary adjunct of this is the unitization of royalty interests, thus bringing all five royalty owners to share in a common royalty pot. Thus, if oil is produced from the single well drilled under unit management, the working interests of the oil companies and the interests of royalty holders are both split five ways. More than one well, obviously, can be drilled, but unit operation applies also to all wells drilled beyond the first.

Great savings can be achieved by unitization, but there are always two sides to a question. Individual interest still counts for much, and it is not always possible to realize the advantages, including the long-term production of larger amounts of oil in a given area, from unitization. But the helter-skelter drilling, production, and other activities in the beginnings of the great Oklahoma City field should rise to haunt those who oppose rational methods in the production of oil.

Doherty's empire is now headed by Alton Jones, as chairman of the board of Cities Service. Under his able leadership the company has grown tremendously. The producing unit of this company has been a great factor in the producing end of the oil industry as a whole. A. W. Ambrose was president for a number of years and was universally recognized as an able executive. After his retirement, Pete (as he was known to many of us) and his wife were victims of an automobile accident while driving from Tulsa to Bartlesville. His successor as president is S. B. Irelan.

The Sunray Oil Corporation, by purchasing and merging different producing and refining companies and properties, and by adding to its own pipe-line division, has, under the able management of F. B. Parriot, Clarence H. Wright, W. C. Whaley, and F. L. Martin, grown into one of the really large integrated independent oil companies.

83

The growth of the Continental Oil Company occupies, in reality, the period of the last quarter century—from the time Continental took over the faltering Marland empire, with Dan Moran, one of the hardest-hitting oil executives in the history of the industry, in the position of main responsibility as president. What drive, efficiency, and imagination can do in the oil business was demonstrated with extraordinary brilliance by Dan, who, like many another top executive, died relatively young. He was succeeded by L. F. McCullum, and the company, with its far-flung holdings and extensive interests, from production and refining to marketing, continues its growth. No traveller to Ponca City, Oklahoma, will fail to be impressed with the evidences of Continental's vast operations there.

In referring to these companies and their development, I am interested less in tipping my hat to contemporaries who, in typically American fashion, have built great properties from small beginnings, than in sketching what I consider a good deal more important. It is organizational qualities, without which the oil industry fails to be an industry at all and could occupy a position no more important than a one-man sluicing operation in the early days of gold. Oil is an extractive industry, to be sure, but the men and companies I have mentioned have helped to give it scope, orderly development, and a destiny closely associated with the best welfare of man.

Money, success, size of operation—these things, I must admit, are important to us all. But more than sixty years of association with oilmen has convinced me that the genuine, fourteen carat oilman is one who thinks and acts in industrial terms, rather than as if he were constantly on the verge of developing a big bonanza. In fact, a good many people who developed bonanzas either failed to realize big profit from them or subsequently went broke.

I think it can be reduced to this: oil began as a game and

has ended up as large-scale industry. In the last half-century I have never been far away from the latter type of development. Maybe I like it best that way.

8

TEAPOT DOME AND BAKU

I REMAINED in charge of our Mexican operations until the latter part of 1921, when I was called to the New York office to look after some special work, but retained my residence in Houston. I returned to the Houston office in 1922. In April of that year I was called to New York again and was told that the Mammoth Oil Company had been organized, that it had obtained a lease on Teapot Dome in Wyoming, and that I was to have charge of the operations. I could move to Denver or to Casper. After my first visit to Casper I decided that this city, which was much closer to the scene of operations than Denver, would be the better place for my office and residence. Accordingly, I moved my family to Casper, where we lived for six years.

I thoroughly enjoyed the people of Casper and acquired among them many lasting friends. Here I met Pat Sullivan, who had been an early mayor of the city and was later a state senator. He was subsequently appointed by Governor Frank Emerson to fill an unexpired term in the United States Senate. I also met E. J. Sullivan, Judge T. Blake Kennedy, and P. C. Spencer. Harry Hynds was among close friends that I made in Wyoming. Charles (Red) Hill, of Denver, who spent much of his time in Wyoming, was another. There too I met W. H. Geiss, a geologist, who later went to Los Angeles, where he attained prominence as an independent oil producer. Other warm friends included James Donoghue, R. S. Shannon, and Fred Goodstein.

When I moved to Casper I had a real job on my hands, and no organization. Frank Algeo was in Casper as manager of the Sinclair interests, which included some production in Salt Creek and at Osage. With his aid I recruited a force. There were twenty-two wells to be started at once. M. J. Delaney, of Dallas, Texas, an old friend of mine from the Ohio days, moved in his Shamrock Drilling Company and went to work. Elmer M. Cooper, of Chanute, Kansas, also moved in a number of drilling tools and did some of the drilling.

The Dome was forty miles from Casper, with only nine miles of paving, and this was on the east half of the road only. The west side was unpaved. This paving, by the way, was the only hard-surface road in Wyoming at that time. We first built four and one-half miles of road from the main Salt Creek road into the Dome, and over fifty miles of telephone line. We then established a temporary camp to house three hundred men. Later we built ten four-room modern houses. We also built two large dormitories and a mess hall to seat 150 at a time, with a suitable kitchen. Next came a warehouse, built on the Chicago and Northwestern Railroad track at Casper, a large warehouse at the Dome, a machine shop, and a large garage. Nearly fifty miles of water and gas lines were laid, buried five feet deep. A sewage-disposal plant was constructed. All of the material needed on the Dome had to be hauled from Casper. Several 55,000-barrel tanks were erected, and a pipe line was laid to Kansas City.

During all this time we were bringing in wells, some good, some fair. The work was started in June. The first organiza-

87

tion that I got together was not up to handling the job in the way I wanted it done. I made many changes and called in Jack Jordan from Homer, Louisiana, and made him superintendent. We had better results from then on. Eventually, I suffered a breakdown and had to leave the job for about four months.

In October, 1922, we drilled in the biggest well ever completed in Wyoming. This was No. 1 on the southwest half of Section 2-38-78, and was the fifteenth well drilled. The well came in unexpectedly at a depth, in shale, of 1,655 feet. It flowed through 1,555 feet of 12½-inch pipe, a solid stream of 41-degree gravity oil. The stream struck the crown-block before it broke. We had no line to the well, and the ground was full of ravines and cracks. Most of the oil was lost. By midnight we had a pipe line to the well, but before we had it connected the well quit flowing. I am positive from tests made by damming up a gully there that the well made at the start over two thousand barrels an hour. It was the biggest well that I have ever seen in the United States, save one, the Lucas gusher at Spindletop, Texas.

Another large well was No. 25, drilled on the northeast part of the Dome. This well came in for over two hundred barrels an hour. It was flowing wild, and we made every effort to shut it in, at the same time scraping a basin to hold the flow. We would pick up the oil from the pond thus formed and pump it into the storage tanks. A team of horses slipped into the pond and drowned. During our efforts to shut the well in there was a terrific rain and electrical storm. The well was making a great amount of gas, which, on account of the rain, settled close to the ground. This greatly increased the danger of explosion and fire from lightning. This well and the big shale well were the only big ones drilled on the Dome. No. 25 was flowing from the Second Wall Creek sand.

While development of Teapot Dome was under way, the

United States government instituted a suit for cancellation of the Mammoth Oil Company lease. Two receivers for the property were appointed by Federal Judge T. Blake Kennedy in his court in Cheyenne. Admiral Joseph Strauss was appointed the Navy representative and Al Watts, Mammoth's representative. I was appointed manager for the receivers.

If you want to know what nerve-wrenching distraction is, just try to obey orders from two receivers with conflicting interests. Admiral Strauss gave up in disgust and resigned. Commander Harry A. Stuart was then named Navy receiver. Stuart was a fine gentleman, and he and I got along well. Stuart wound up his career as an admiral. The Navy had another official on the ground in the person of Commander W. H. Osgood, who filled the post of observer. He was quite fair, and the four of us—Watts, Stuart, Osgood, and I had no great difficulty in working together smoothly.

The first trial of the suit for cancellation of the lease was before Judge Kennedy, at Cheyenne, and it was decided in favor of the Mammoth Oil Company. An appeal was taken by the government to the Circuit Court of Appeals at St. Paul, Minnesota. This court reversed the opinion of Judge Kennedy. Mammoth Oil Company appealed to the United States Supreme Court. The Supreme Court, in 1927, upheld the Circuit Court decision that the lease to the Mammoth Oil Company was illegal and subject to cancellation.

We were ordered to close the receivership and turn the lease over to the Navy. All of the tanks, pipe lines, buildings, wells, and equipment went with the lease, and at midnight on December 31, 1927, Teapot Dome was shut down, probably like grandfather's clock, "never to run again." So ended nearly six years' expenditures of money, time, and effort. Incidentally, the receivers paid into the court over $3,000,000.

Before the receivership was established, I had suffered the breakdown already mentioned and had been advised by my doctors to take a trip away from Casper. The altitude, about 5,200 feet, was producing a nervous condition. Mrs. Connelly and I, Mr. and Mrs. Elmer M. Cooper, and my secretary, Margaret Dougherty, left for Texas. After a short time in Houston, we went to Mexico City for three weeks, then to Tampico, where we spent ten days. We next took a trip on our tanker, the *A. E. Watts,* and went to Havana, where we spent two weeks more. By this time I was feeling fine. We went to New York, then to Washington, where our children were in school, and then back to Casper. We were there only a short time when we made our first trip to Yellowstone Park.

While in Wyoming I organized the Repollo Oil Company, to function as a wildcat operator. I selected three or four names, but the secretary of state rejected each because of its similarity to a name already adopted by some other company. I often have been asked how I came to hit upon the name eventually approved. Here is the answer: the company's auditor in Wyoming was Sinclair Reekie; the treasurer was W. W. Pollock. Using part of the name of each of these men, I came out with "Repollo." The company was merged later with the Sinclair Wyoming Oil Company, which in turn was merged into the Sinclair Oil and Gas Company.

Also while I was living in Casper, the Rocky Mountain Oil and Gas Association was organized in 1922. Among those attending the first meeting, held in the office of the Consolidated Royalty Company, were former Governor B. B. Brooks, Clarence Richardson, E. J. Sullivan, James P. Kem (later United States senator from Missouri), M. J. Foley, Bob Ellison, and myself. Brooks was elected president, and I vice president.

This organization, starting with a dozen or so names on its roll, now has a membership of several hundred, exerting an important influence in its field. In view of the development which already has taken place in the Rocky Mountain states and the further development in prospect, the association could easily become the largest of its kind.

The fact that I am still alive and writing this account at the age of eighty-one cannot be traced to any tranquillity in the Casper years. I have outlined briefly the main course of events between 1922 and 1927. In the midst of these busy times, in May, 1923, I received a wire from Al Watts asking me to come to New York as soon as possible. I left that same afternoon and stopped between trains in Toledo and ordered a suit of clothes.

On my arrival in New York I reported to Watts's office. He said that Harry Sinclair wanted to see me at once. When I called on Sinclair his greeting was, "Have you a passport?"

"I knew that New York was fast filling with foreigners," I replied, "but I hadn't heard it was necessary to have a passport to enter."

"It is not so bad as that," laughed Sinclair, "but we are leaving on Saturday for Europe, and you are to be one of the party. We will arrange for passports tomorrow morning. Watts will give you all the necessary information about the trip."

This was on Thursday at about 11 A. M., and we were to leave on the *Homeric* at 10 o'clock Saturday forenoon. Our children were in school in Washington. I made arrangements for them to come to New York that afternoon, to be with me at my sailing. Watts was unable to say how long we would be gone, but believed it would be at least two months.

I called Mrs. Connelly in Casper and told her of the European trip. It would be impossible for her to get to New York before we sailed. I had quite a bit of shopping to do, as I had come to New York with only a small wardrobe. I called the tailor in Toledo and told him I had to have that suit by Saturday morning. He promised it, and it was delivered to me at 2 A. M. Saturday.

91

Friday was a hectic day getting ready. Part of the morning was taken up in getting the passports, and the rest of the time was devoted to shopping. I foolishly bought a trunk. Never again in all the sea voyages I made did I ever burden myself with one. After taking that confounded trunk as far as Paris I stored it there, to be picked up on my return.

On the trip for the Sinclair interests were Harry F. Sinclair, Elisha Walker, A. E. Watts, William S. Mowris, Archie Roosevelt, Thomas W. White, Grattan Stanford, Rod Crandall, I, and a male secretary. Also in the party were Bill Loucks, Bob Law, and Mason Day, these three representing the Barnsdall International Oil Company.

Not until we were aboard the ship did I learn the whole purpose of the journey. The Russian government had confiscated all oil properties owned by foreign companies and was operating them for the government. Mason Day had obtained from the Russians a contract giving a number of concessions in the Baku area to the Barnsdall International Oil Company. In accordance with an agreement which Day had made with Sinclair, our company was to take an interest with Barnsdall. Some of us were to visit Baku, inspect these leases, and start the drilling of some wells.

We landed at Southampton and proceeded to London. We spent two weeks in London, always keeping in touch with a Russian named Krassin, who represented the Soviet government there. We had plenty of time to visit places of interest in and around London. We crossed the Channel and spent several days in Paris.

It should be explained here that the weeks spent in sightseeing were no part of the plans formulated before we left New York. And developments revealed that our party need not have been in such a feverish rush to sail from home. Russia was our destination, but we could not go to that country until we received word that Soviet officials were ready for us.

So we decided that instead of cooling our heels in a London hotel we might as well see points of interest within easy reach.

Tom White and I, with ancestral roots in Ireland, decided that here was an opportunity to visit the island, for which we both entertained a warm feeling. None of the rest of the party went. We landed at Kingston early on a Sunday morning. The customs officials examined our baggage. We were then searched for arms. As a soldier who was to search me approached, we both laughed. He was at least 6 feet 6 inches tall. I am 5 feet 5. I suggested that he give me a box to stand on. As I had no weapons, the search was soon over.

Monday we spent doing Dublin. On Tuesday morning I took a train to Newry, in County Down, northern Ireland. The Newry River, dividing line at that point between southern and northern Ireland, was fortified on both sides with barricades of sandbags. Both sides bristled with soldiers. The hostile feeling between these two sections of Ireland at that period was the cause of the warlike preparations.

In Newry I hired a Dodge car and a driver and drove to Burren Chapel, the ancestral home of the Connelly family. Burren Chapel is a small hamlet. We stopped our car at a small grocery and notion store. A girl sat on the store porch. "Are there any Connellys around here?" I asked.

"Glory be to God, there's nothing but Connellys and their relations!" she cried. "I'm one."

With such a prospect confronting me, I decided to seek out the nearest related Connelly whose name had been given me, an Owen Connelly, and I inquired for him. My friend on the porch said he lived down the road about a mile. Before we reached his home we saw three men at a gravel pit. Two were working and one was looking on. I made a mental bet that the one looking on was a relation. We stopped the car, and I asked if they knew Owen Connelly. The watcher came over to the car and said, "I am Owen Connelly." I won my bet.

93

Owen got into the car with us and we drove to his home, which was small but comfortable. His wife made tea and served it with small cakes. A man named McCoy, who had married a sister of Owen's, lived across the road. We visited his home. McCoy claimed to be one hundred years old, but his sight was so good he wore no glasses. He said he knew my grandfather and grandmother, who had left Ireland in 1842 for the United States.

We drove down the road about a mile, where McCoy showed me an iron gate hung on a stone post. This gate was at a lane which entered the grounds of my great-grandfather's place. The ruins of a stone house of fair size were still there. McCoy said that my great-grandfather was a "gentlemin" who had race horses, wore a silk hat, and carried a gold-headed cane. At one time he had owned four hundred acres of land and a linen mill at Warren's Point. The mill had been taxed out of business by the English. (Taxes entered the economic picture in those days too.)

While we were at this gate, which was called "Billy's Gate," McCoy asked me if I had ever heard the story of my great-grandfather's bull. I told him I had listened to a lot of bull in many places, but not in Ireland. McCoy explained that the place where we stood was in northern Ireland and that one July 12, which is Orangemen's Day, a parade of Orangemen came past the farm with banners flying, wearing scarlet coats, and with a band playing. Great-grandfather had a blooded bull in the pasture. The bull, excited by the band and angered by the scarlet coats, jumped the fence, charged into the parade, and injured some of the marchers. McCoy continued, "And almost every Sunday after that, for a long time, the Catholics in the area around the farm would come to look at Billy Connelly's 'papal bull.' "

We visited the graves of my great-grandfather and great-grandmother and those of other relatives of less remote gen-

erations. In all, I had an eventful day. I returned to Dublin
that evening, and later that night I took the boat from Kingston back to Wales, and a train to London.

When all of us had reassembled in London, we learned of
the plans for the Russian trip. Sinclair, Stanford, Walker,
Loucks, Law, Day, and the secretary were to go directly to
Moscow. The others, including Cliff Longshore, who had
joined us in London, were to head for Batum.

On leaving the United States we had no visas on our passports for Russia; we were told by the State Department that
we would enter that country on our own responsibility. The
United States at that time had no diplomatic relations with
the Soviets.

Krassin had finally informed us that we could leave for
Russia, so on June 23 we left London for Calais, France,
where we boarded the Oriental Limited for Constantinople.
Watts and Mowris got aboard the wrong train but rejoined
us in Paris. We went from Switzerland into Italy through the
Simplon Tunnel. Our first stop in Italy was at Milan, where
we went sightseeing for several hours. Just before we arrived
at Milan two of our bright boys conceived the brilliant idea of
hiding their money in the railroad coach. They took the cover
off a small recess in the side of the coach and put their money
in it, then screwed the cover back into place.

As we approached the station after our tour of the city,
we saw a train moving out. Someone yelled, "That's our
train!" We all rushed through the station, through a baggage
car, and scrambled onto the train. Still panting from our wild
dash, we discovered it was not our train. An engine was
merely switching a few cars. On getting off we were accosted
by gendarmes, who demanded the reason for our mad race.
It took some time to find an interpreter who could explain
our hurry. We were told to go and sin no more. As soon as we
got back on our own train the money which had been so

cleverly cached was hastily removed from its hiding place.

After arriving in Constantinople, we spent several days futilely endeavoring to obtain passage on a ship to Batum. Our days of waiting were filled with sightseeing in this ancient and thoroughly cosmopolitan city. Before the first World War, Constantinople was overrun by thousands of stray dogs, protected from death by the Moslems. When the Germans came, they started cleaning up the city. They gathered up hordes of these dogs and moved them to an island near by. A plague of cats then infested the city, and when we were there the streets and walks were overrun with them. They carried fleas, which discovered in me a special dainty. After every trip outdoors I had to apply all my cunning to the task of catching the little demons. Watts insisted on painting the bites with iodine, with the result that I became so spotted that a leopard would have envied me.

After all our efforts to find a boat had proved fruitless, we were told by Admiral Bristol, the United States commissioner to Turkey, that he was sending a destroyer on a practice trip, and that it might as well go to Batum as anywhere else. He put us aboard the destroyer *Gilmer,* which after forty hours landed us at Batum.

It was July 4. News that a United States naval vessel was coming to the dock had spread, and a crowd was on hand to see us land. Among the gathering was an American named Anderson, from Syracuse, N.Y., in charge of the Near East Relief station in Batum. He was as glad to see us as though we owed him money.

During the afternoon we took in what there was to see in Batum, at that time a city of about fifty thousand population, on the eastern shore of the Black Sea. It is the capital of Adzhar, an autonomous socialist Soviet republic. The Russians had a large installation of storage tanks and pumps located there. It is the western end of the pipe line from Baku.

We spent the greater part of two days examining this installation and then boarded a train for Baku.

We of course were not familiar with train customs in Russia, and this ignorance caused us some annoyance. Bill Mowris and I went into a compartment, planning to take both the lower and upper berths. While we were talking, two old women climbed into the upper berth with their baggage. All this time they were talking to Mowris and me, in Russian presumably, though it might have been Turkish or Greek so far as we knew.

Anderson, who was still on the platform, came to our aid. He told us that had we been sitting in the two berths we could have held them, but that as the women had taken the upper berth we were out. I told Bill to take the lower and I would bunk somewhere else. All of the berths were taken. Several of our fellows offered to give up their berths, but I went back to the first compartment and sat on the lower berth with Mowris until it was time to turn in. Having borrowed several steamer rugs from the other fellows, I made a bed on the floor.

The railroad track was rough, and both of the old women became carsick. That night stands out as one of the most unpleasant in my life. Adding to the bitterness of my dark mood was the fact that I had $5,000 with me, and here I was trying to sleep in a traveling pigpen. Bill and I were certainly glad to see daylight. We got out on the rear platform of the train and drew some clean air into our lungs.

The first place of importance at which we stopped was Tiflis, the capital of Georgia, another Soviet republic. Our train was held up here for several hours. In fact, the ride from Batum to Baku, on a dirty, unsanitary train, took forty-eight hours. With intense relief we left the foul, malodorous coaches at Baku, which was the center of the Russian oil industry.

Upon our arrival at Baku we went to the Roma Hotel. The members of the party now were Watts, Mowris, Roosevelt, White, Crandall, George Lord, Al Miller, Elbert Isom, and I. Lord, Miller, and Isom had joined us at Batum.

Our quarters at the hotel were on the top floor, and they comprised a string of connecting rooms. There was only one bathroom on the floor. There were no screens on the windows, nor could we buy anything to use as a substitute. If we used a light in a room, the room was immediately filled with all kinds of flying pests, so when we spent an evening inside it was in the dark.

Whenever members of our party left the hotel, they were trailed by secret police. There would be one secret policeman for each member of our party. This continued all the time that we were in Baku. When we visited an oil field our shadows came along. One day we used two "speeders" on the railroad to visit a pump station. About forty miles out of Baku two other speeders began trailing us. We had taken lunches with us, but when we were ready to eat we changed our minds. The lunches smelled too high. We turned them over to our shadows, who ate them with gusto. We afterwards heard that two of the men became violently sick that night.

We spent nearly three weeks in and around Baku visiting the different oil fields, refineries, and other installations. Our guide on these trips was a Russian Jew named Edelstein. He could speak English, and he became a helpful and companionable member of the party. His title of "boring master" was embroidered on his cap. All wells were guarded by soldiers, and Edelstein was not permitted to go onto a lease unless he wore his cap.

Edelstein invited our party for dinner one evening, asking us to choose between 7 and 10 o'clock as the hour. He explained that before the revolution he had owned a comfortable home, but that the government had taken it over and had moved another family in with his. The kitchen and dining room thereafter were used in common. The other family, he

The oil dudes who went to Baku and were thrown for a loss. *Left to right:* W. S. Mowris, W. L. Connelly, A. E. Watts, Thomas W. White, at Batum, July 4, 1923.

Above, left: What sometimes happens when a big well goes wild: Lago Petroleum Corporation's Punta Benitez Well No. 148 in Lake Maracaibo, Venezuela, pouring oil at thousands of barrels per day, after demolishing the drilling equipment, only to disappear subsequently in a crater, January, 1928. *Above, right:* Andrew McKenzie, W. L. Connelly, and Joe Waldo sizing up the location for first well drilled by Venezuela Petroleum Corporation in Venezuela, February, 1929—it was a dry hole. *Below:* When the roads weren't rough in the oil business, they were often wet. Fording a river in Venezuela, 1929.

explained, would allow him to choose the hour for our dinner. We selected 10 o'clock. We had a good dinner, prepared and served by Edelstein's wife and daughter, who did not dine with us.

Edelstein also had a small house on the shore of the Caspian Sea. He invited us there for a dinner and overnight stay. We rode in autos to within a couple of miles of his house. The sand was too deep for the cars to get closer. All but Mowris were given mules to ride the rest of the way. Mowris was given a gig, with a horse drawing it, and he drove in style. We had an excellent meal and spent a delightful evening. As the house was small, Edelstein had placed cots in a shed for us. Except for being crowded, we had an enjoyable experience.

Edelstein had a daughter who was with the Metropolitan Opera Company in New York. Neither he nor his wife was allowed to write to her. When we arrived back in New York we gave her several letters that had been entrusted to us. I heard later that Edelstein had been shot by order of the government. He was accused of having given certain information to the Shell Oil Company.

We had many meetings with the local chapter of the oil industry's governing body. This chapter had three members— a machinist, a carpenter, and a sailor. The sailor was chairman. These were the men with whom we had to discuss oil operations. Try to imagine the maddening job we faced in trying to make them understand what we were talking about. Edelstein was really a life and time saver here.

We spent a large portion of each day visiting oil pools and refineries. All of the equipment, both in the field and at the refineries, was in poor condition. There had been no replacements of any kind during the war.

The oil-field workers were Russians, Persians, and Tartars. Most of the drillers were Persians. As I remember, they were paid about fifteen dollars (in terms of United States money) a month. In addition they were given an allowance of tobacco and black bread. Baku's refineries, pipe lines, tank cars, tankers, and oil wells were the property of the Soviet government, following their confiscation from private owners. Among the former owners was the Shell Oil Company.

While we were in Baku, the Barnsdall International Oil Company made a deal for the drilling of two wells in one of the pools not far from Baku. These wells were later drilled, but they were taken over by the Russians. This, fundamentally, was the principal consequence of a long, toilsome, and expensive expedition. It is always difficult to understand a government in an industrial role, but a communist government so occupied was doubly so for us. We had simply made the mistake of believing that an engagement by the Russians to permit us to produce at Baku would be honored. It wasn't. We got paid for completing two wells, but that was all.

The work for which we had been sent to Russia having been completed, our party began to break up. Watts and Roosevelt went to Moscow. Lord, Miller, and Isom left for Constantinople by way of Tiflis and Batum. They encountered difficulty in getting away from Batum and were delayed there for about ten days before their passports were visaed so that they could leave Russia. The rest of the party, in contrast, had no trouble. White, Longshore, and I remained in Baku for some days after the others had left. The three of us then boarded a train for Moscow.

This trip required three and one-half days and three nights. The sleeping cars were clean and comfortable, and the dining-car service was fairly good. Though long in hours and miles, the trip had its compensations. We passed through some fairly large towns and many villages. There were no buildings on the farms. The peasants live in villages located at the center of the farming communities, and go to and from the farms. This practice, we were told, was adopted to afford

100

greater safety from raids of roaming Tartars in earlier years.

Our trip took us through the Ukraine, famous for its agriculture. We passed close enough to the Sea of Azov to get a glimpse of it. We arrived in Moscow on a Sunday evening in a violent wind and rain storm.

The Russians placed at our disposal a house which provided much better accommodations than we could have obtained at a hotel. It had belonged to a banker who had been "liquidated" by the government, with confiscation of his property. The house, a large one of about fifteen rooms, was well furnished and comfortable, but had only one bathroom, a small one. A butler, chef, and many other servants were at our service. This staff was changed completely every three days. We surmised that this was done either because the servants were to spy on us or because the government was fearful that we might obtain secret information if we had time to make friends of the servants. In any event, we were well taken care of while in Moscow.

Few foreigners were living in Moscow at that time. The United States had no representative there. We saw one American during our stay. This was "Big Bill" Haywood, of I.W.W. fame. I understand that he was later expelled from Russia and finished his days in Constantinople. The city was well lighted, had well-paved streets and many fine buildings, and was up-to-date in all ways. Many of the buildings showed the effects of the civil war which had raged there.

When we applied for the visas for our passports, so that we could start for home, we were told that ordinarily this would mean a delay of at least two weeks. We were given particular consideration, and the job was done in about twenty-four hours. We were then free to leave Russia. Sleeping cars not being available, we took a day coach for Riga, the capital of Latvia, and from thence we went to Rotterdam, London, and New York, where Mrs. Connelly met me.

9

SINCLAIR ENTERS VENEZUELA

IN DECEMBER, 1928, the Sinclair Consolidated Oil Corporation acquired a majority interest in the stock of the Venezuelan Petroleum Company, and the following were elected officers: H. R. Kunhardt, Jr., chairman of the board; W. L. Connelly, president; J. Fletcher Farrell, vice president and treasurer; M. L. Gosney, vice president and assistant treasurer; P. W. Thirtle, vice president and comptroller; W. B. Heroy and W. S. Mowris, vice presidents.

Venezuelan Petroleum had royalty interest under Gulf Oil Company leases in Lake Maracaibo and held concessions from the Venezuelan government on many thousands of hectares. These concessions had to be evaluated, those that seemingly had merit to be retained and the others to be surrendered. To start this work, W. B. Heroy and I made a trip to Venezuela in January, 1929. Besides being a vice president of the company, Heroy was a geologist of note. We left New York on January 16 on the Red D Line steamer *Caracas*. Edgar Pew, of the Sun Oil Company, was among the passengers. On January 21 we anchored at San Juan, Puerto Rico, and while the ship was unloading and loading cargo we spent several hours sightseeing. We visited Moro Castle, the university, and a number of state buildings. The people were clean and comfortably dressed.

We left the same day for La Guaira, Venezuela. No little excitement developed when a small boat was sighted adrift. Our captain swung the *Caracas* out of its course to investigate. But no one was aboard the drifting boat, so the inevitable question of what had become of its passengers remained. We arrived at La Guaira early on the morning of January 23— seven days out of New York. Now it is done in about twelve hours from Miami, Florida, by air.

At La Guaira we were joined by Andrew N. MacKenzie, the company manager in Venezuela. MacKenzie had worked for me as a geologist on Teapot Dome. We drove from La Guaira to Caracas over a road which was a succession of twists and curves. The road distance was twenty-eight miles; by air, eight. We registered at the Middleton Hotel. As I walked into the lobby I met Joel Lipscomb, an attorney for the Atlantic Oil Company with whom I had been well acquainted in Tampico, Mexico. I met many other old friends and acquaintances from Tampico during my stay in Caracas. Among them was Gene Templeton, a former geologist for Sinclair, whom I had last seen in Moscow, Russia.

Our Venezuelan offices were in Valencia, about 110 miles from Caracas. The drive was over good roads, kept in top shape, possibly for the reason that the president of Venezuela spent much of his time in Valencia and made the trip between Caracas and that city often.

We desired first to make a trip to Maracaibo and view the Gulf's producing leases in Lake Maracaibo. Heroy, MacKenzie, and I drove to Puerto Cabello, a seaport. Here we saw the navy yard and a prison where most of the political offenders were confined. We left by boat about midnight for Wilhelmstadt, on the Island of Curaçao, Dutch West Indies.

We spent two days on this island and left for Maracaibo, where we arrived the next morning.

Chester Cribbs, who was in charge of the Gulf's interests in this part of Venezuela, met us at the dock, assisted us through the customs, and then took us to his camp, where we were guests of the Gulf. While in the living room at Cribbs's home we were treated to a mild earthquake. Windows shook, dishes rattled, and the floor swayed. No large damage was done, however.

The situation in Venezuelan oil production when we came to that country was roughly as follows:

Oil seeps had been known and exploited in a primitive way in the vicinity of Maracaibo from prehistoric times. It was not until a year or two preceding World War I, however, that production in any determined way had been undertaken. But by 1920 Venezuela was ascending fast among oil-producing countries—especially since revolutionary disturbances in Mexico had caused many producing and refining companies to proceed cautiously in the latter country. In the late twenties (the time of our arrival), Venezuela had moved up to second position among the world's oil nations, only the U.S. surpassing her.

The Lake Maracaibo area was a well-proven, heavy-producing field. We had, as I have indicated, royalty interests there, but it seemed to the Sinclair companies, and especially to its geologists, that the part of good sense dictated explorations in the interior and away from the already heavily exploited Maracaibo basin. This we proposed to do on the current trip, directing principal attention to our own concessions.

Let us say here that our trip forecast some of the difficulties to be met in future oil operations in this rugged, overgrown country, and confirmed some of the already-known problems that had been encountered by other producers who had preceded us.

104

On January 30 we left the Gulf camp in a launch furnished by Cribbs and spent several hours visiting the Ambrosia, La Rosa, and Lagunillas fields in the lake. A strange sight to us was a tanker loading oil at docks surrounded by derricks, tanks, and boiler stations, on foundations in water. This was long before off-shore drilling in the Gulf of Mexico. It was 9:30 that night before we returned to the camp.

We drove into Maracaibo the next morning and called on C. C. McDermond, a friend of Tampico days. Mac was handling a scouting service, providing news of interest to companies having concessions in that part of Venezuela. We drove to a concession in Larrain and made a location for a well; we also drove to a location for a well of the Union Oil Company in the same vicinity.

On February 3 we left Maracaibo on a Gulf launch for Altagracia, where we were met by a truck in which our baggage was to be hauled, and a small car in which we were to drive across Venezuela, visiting several concessions and ending our trip at Maturin. The trip, with stops at camps and for interviews with geologists and torsion-balance crews (geophysics had entered oil explorations in the late twenties) took us eighteen days. Counting side trips, it covered nearly two thousand miles over some of the worst roads in any country.

The first night out we spent at the camp of the Richmond Oil Company, where we had an excellent dinner and a good bed. After an early breakfast we resumed our drive, which was to carry us during the day into the Andes Mountains. The roads were well made but narrow and characterized by very steep grades, with drops of one hundred to one thousand feet.

We spent that night in Uriche, in a native hotel. We had brought hammocks for sleeping, as few hotels in the small towns and villages had beds. Hooks had been screwed into the walls, and we hung the hammocks from them. Doors were

105

left open, and frogs, toads, dogs, chickens, and other representatives of barnyard life wandered in at will. If a hen hopped onto your face to investigate its possibilities as a roosting place, you brushed it off with whatever accompaniment of language you might feel appropriate.

Notwithstanding these tranquilizing conditions, I was restless that night and tumbled out of my hammock. I landed on a pig, which squealed lustily and struggled to get out from under me. I yelled and called the pig unkind names, at the same time fighting with passionate zeal to separate myself from the animal. Every time I tried to break away, the pig apparently was seized with a wild impulse to lunge in the same direction. As a result, we bumped around in a maddening stalemate.

Then dogs began to bark. Other creatures added squawks, quacks, cackles, and yelps to the nocturnal clamor. Heroy, MacKenzie, and Elder (our truck driver) leaped from their hammocks in the raucous confusion and wanted to know what was the matter. Eventually the pig and I managed to dissolve our ill-starred association, and quiet was restored.

We were on the road by 7 o'clock the next morning. We had some mountain driving on fair roads. After taking lunch at the Universal Hotel in Barquisimeto, we continued our trip and crossed several rivers, most of them showing only a trickle. During the day we passed from the state of Lara into the state of Portuguesa, and at nightfall reached Espino. Our hotel beds had no mattresses, so we put blankets on the springs.

The next morning we again hit the road early and drove to Guanare for breakfast. Later we forded the Portuguesa River, after MacKenzie had waded into it to locate a crossing, and then in succession we forded six rivers and were ferried across the Rio Bocono. The roads all day were bad. Late in the afternoon we reached Barinas, the capital of the state of

Zamora. The town had about two thousand people, but was said to have had nearly fifty thousand at one time. I cannot see why. Marquis Bocono, the Spanish governor of the district, who died in 1811, is buried there. We had headquarters for several geological parties and a torsion-balance party in Barinas.

The next morning MacKenzie, Waldo, one of our geologists, and I drove to Barinitas, a hamlet not far from the camp. Here a structure had been located, a suggested location for a well had been recommended, and thus we drilled our first well in Venezuela.

On February 10 MacKenzie, Heroy, and I, with Elder driving, left in a small car to return to the office in Valencia. Out of camp only a short distance we slid off the crossing in the Santa Domingo River. After trying for some time to get out under our own power, and failing, Elder walked back to camp, got a truck and driver, and pulled us out. During this day we again forded six rivers and were ferried across one. It was 2 A. M., February 11, before we arrived at Valencia— nineteen hours on the road.

We spent the next day in the office there. Then MacKenzie, Heroy, Elder, and I drove to Caracas. Here we spent two days with our attorney and visiting some of the Venezuelan officials, whose cordial interest in our operations made our stay a pleasant one and greatly facilitated our future work.

We then returned to Valencia. Driving through the city we saw President Juan Vicente Gómez and an escort. Later in the day we left Valencia for El Sombrero, and on to Maturin. On this part of our trip we were repeatedly requested to show our passports and our vaccination certificates. There were numerous cases of smallpox in the country. Again we slept in hammocks, but with no tumbles or pigs to enliven the journey. In fact, nearly all of our nights until we reached Maturin were spent in hammocks. The next day we left El

Sombrero without breakfast. We had but one meal during the day and that one at about 11 o'clock. The night was spent at the Americano Hotel at Larazoza. The next day we drove to Barcelona. We had been stuck for some time in sand and also in a river. We had a good hotel here, with good food. The following day we drove to Maturin, where we were guests of the Creole Petroleum Corporation at its staff house, and we were made very comfortable.

The Creole Petroleum Corporation was then, and remains today, the largest producer of oil in Venezuela and one of the largest producers in the world. It is a subsidiary of the Standard Oil Company of New Jersey.

The next day, accompanied by representatives of the Creole, we drove to that company's property at Quire-Quire. There were two wells in this field producing 16-degree oil. One "blew in" at a depth of 2,338 feet and was good for 2,000 barrels. It sanded up and could not be made to produce more than 300 barrels after being worked over. The other was making about 300 barrels from a depth of 3,343 feet. A third well was drilling, and a rig was being built for a fourth. The driller on tower had worked for me in Oklahoma. The drive was through a country of wonderful scenery. We returned to Maturin for the night. The next day was spent in visiting mud volcanoes and the Venezuelan Petroleum leases in the vicinity of Maturin.

We were on the road early the next day, on our return to Barcelona, where, after pulling a Gulf scout out of a river, we were in turn stuck and pulled out by a truck.

Then on February 21, eighteen days after our overland travels began, we were ready to depart. We left Barcelona before breakfast and drove to Guanita, where we had breakfast about 7 o'clock. Here we parted company with Elder and the car. He returned to Valencia. We took the *Commewigne* and sailed for Port of Spain, Island of Trinidad. From there we progressed by easy stages, visiting a number of the Caribbean islands, to New York.

Though the trip was a hard one in many ways—bad roads, poor food and beds, and much nasty weather—I felt well repaid. Unpleasant incidents are to be expected in the life of an oilman, at home and abroad, and I gained valuable knowledge concerning South America and our holdings there. The Venezuelan Petroleum Company was to obtain substantial production from its concessions in Venezuela in later years. As for the Republic of Venezuela, I can only say that many of its splendid cities—Caracas and Maracaibo notable among them—reflected then the importance and benefits great petroleum resources had conferred. In the years since, as any South American traveler knows, Venezuela has witnessed great development, so that these same cities, and the country as a whole, for that matter, are among the best and most forward-looking—as well as the wealthiest—in the Western Hemisphere.

10

STRANGE PLACES
AND STRANGER PEOPLE

On July 26, 1929, I embarked on an adventurous journey which was to introduce me to strange places, stranger people, and exciting scenes. It was to embrace the refinement of cultured European homes and the heathenish rites of naked tribesmen in the remote recesses of Africa.

Accompanied by Mrs. Connelly, our daughter Elizabeth, our son Harry, and my secretary, Miss Margaret Dougherty, I sailed from New York on the *Homeric,* of the White Star Line, for Europe. From there I was to go to Angola, West Africa, a distance of four thousand miles, on a slow boat.

The purpose of this trip was twofold: to tour some of the countries and cities of Europe with my family, and to transact some business. The Compania de Petroleo de Angola had obtained an oil concession on forty million acres of land in Angola. The Sinclair Consolidated Oil Corporation had a large stock interest in this company and had charge of the operation. Several wells had been drilled, but no oil in commercial quantities had as yet been unearthed. Since the drilling of the last well, the company geologists had done more work and had recommended that a well be drilled on a newly discovered anticline. The stock holdings, other than Sinclair's, were in the hands of Belgian and Portuguese groups. I was to call on these people in Brussels, Belgium, and Lisbon, Portugal, explain to them that we desired to drill another well, and ask for their consent—also get their share of the funds required for this further effort at production.

We landed at Cherbourg, France, and spent several weeks sightseeing in that country, Switzerland, and Belgium. In Paris I was in touch with Harry A. Hassan, our Paris representative; and in Brussels, with Richard M. Gross, our representative in Belgium. Aside from business matters, we had splendid visits at both places through the cordial attentiveness of these men and their families. Harry Hassan has since become a Sinclair vice president at Houston, and Dick Gross is now treasurer of the Richfield Oil Corporation in Los Angeles.

After I had left for Africa, the others toured England, Ireland, and Scotland, then returned home.

While in Brussels, I had made reservations on the Blue Star Liner *Avalona* for Lisbon. I was told that the boat train would leave London for Tilbury at noon. At about 10:30 A. M., after reaching London, I went to the office of Thomas Cook and Sons to pick up my tickets, which I had paid for in Brussels. I was informed the boat train had left for Tilbury at 10 o'clock and that I had missed my boat. There ensued a lively exchange of strong language, with the Cook force at the receiving end most of the time.

I persuaded the office manager to put one of the higher-up clerks in a taxi with me for a quick drive to Tilbury in an effort to catch the ship. All insisted that it was a foolish attempt, that the boat would be gone. They refused to phone a request that the ship be held until I arrived. On the ensuing run to the docks, I am confident that the taxi driver never made a faster trip through London than he made that day.

We arrived at the dock just in time to see the *Avalona* steaming out of the harbor. A motorboat was lying at the dock. The Cook clerk and I piled in and told the boatman to overtake the liner. While we were racing through the water, the clerk and I stood up in the boat and waved and shouted. Finally someone on the *Avalona* noticed us, and the steamer was slowed down. Our motorboat ran alongside. A line was lowered for my baggage, a Jacob's ladder was lowered for me, and I climbed aboard while the liner was still under way.

The following appeared in the *London News* of August 15, 1929: "An American businessman caught the Blue Star Liner *Avalona* at Tilbury today by engaging a taxi in London and catching up with the liner when she was under way in a motor launch."

The man from Cook's who had accompanied me to Tilbury and had seen me board the liner called on Mrs. Connelly at the Hyde Park Hotel to tell her about my adventure. She had in her hands a copy of the *London News* and had just read the item telling of the unconventional fashion in which I had caught the liner.

The captain invited me to sit at his table during the trip, declaring that anyone making the fight that I had to board his ship was entitled to recognition. Of course I accepted. I had to make that ship, for I had an important engagement in Lisbon with some of our partners in the African development.

I was busy while in Lisbon, an old and delightful city, but friends saw that I visited most of the interesting spots. During my stay, while waiting for a ship to Africa, I met two young Swiss fliers who were about to take off in an airplane for New York. I gave them a letter of introduction to Al Watts. The letter never was presented. The two airmen, about nineteen or twenty years old, were lost at sea on the flight.

On August 20 I left on the steamer Mozambique for Angola. With me was a rig builder, who was to use native help in erecting the drilling derrick. While we were still in the Tagus River one of a group of prisoners who were being transported to Angola for long terms jumped into the water in an attempt to escape. He was pulled out by a man in a fishing boat and was returned to our ship. He did escape later, however, while we were anchored at the Island of Madeira.

The first days of our trip were in heavy weather, and the boat rolled violently, but I was not bothered. By this time I was a pretty fair traveler. Yet, in spite of periodic stops—at Madeira in two days, at San Thome in eleven—this was not my idea of fun. The boat was making only nine knots an hour, and the trip was deadly monotonous. There were none of the forms of entertainment that ordinarily are provided on a transatlantic voyage.

Finally, on September 4, we anchored off Luanda at 9:30 A.M. My rig builder and I were met at the ship by Walt Small, our manager; Captain de Barros, the concession attorney; and our office manager, José Barradas. Customs officials were courteous. We had a nice house at the camp and a clean eating house. Arthur C. Veatch, Sinclair's chief geologist, came in from the bush that evening.

We made our first trip into the bush to Cacoba Dome, where we had made a location to drill a well. Brown, the rig builder; Cranford, a mechanic; Veatch; and Small accompanied me. We crossed the Cuanza River in a steel power boat. Our land conveyance was a truck, which had hard springs. The road to Cacoba, where we crossed the river, was, moreover, vile. But Cacoba Dome looked good to us, and that, really, was why we were taking this beating.

On the way back to camp, where we arrived after dark, I found myself wondering rather sourly how many thousands of miles I had been bounced about on wretched caricatures of roads on oil business in Pennsylvania, Ohio, West Virginia, Indiana, Illinois, Kansas, Oklahoma, Louisiana, Wyoming,

Montana, Utah, New Mexico, Mexico, Russia, Venezuela—and now in Africa! Were there no good roads in the world?

Despite Cacoba Dome, I could not confine my interest to oil alone. Here were people like none I had ever seen before, of course—black as night, living in villages like those that evidently had been in use for centuries, pursuing game and small farming, with maize as one of the principal crops and a staple of diet. Their dwellings were of thatch, and on the coastal plain they needed every bit of protection from the sun possible, for the tropical rays there were murderous. The interior is, in the main, a more hospitable place for these natives and for the limited white population of Angola. The plateau there is from 3,500 to nearly 6,000 feet in elevation.

We used natives for a variety of tasks during this trip of exploration and location. One was said to have been a cannibal. He looked the part. The women were like women everywhere, resourceful and durable. Like American Indians, they carried children slung on their backs. They and their men wore clothes enough, but simple ones, to cover their nakedness. I should guess, from information gathered in several quarters, that there were more than two and one-half million blacks in Angola when we made our trip.

The country is vast for this population—pretty close to five hundred thousand square miles—situated on the west coast of Africa, southwest of the Belgian Congo. It contained then an abundance of game—buffalo, zebra, sable antelope, roan antelope, giraffe, leopard, and lion. It has since become of considerable importance as a producer of cotton, coffee, sisal, and corn, as well as diamonds, which were perhaps the most valuable of its mineral resources in 1929. Its oil is of no consequence, but more of that later.

During our stay, Veatch, Captain de Barros, Small, and I called on the high commissioner for Angola. He received us graciously and provided refreshments. The commissioner im-

114

Harry F. Sinclair, 1944.

Excluding the man on the left, some of the Big Brass, 1949. *Left to right:* W. L. Connelly, P. W. Thirtle, P. C. Spencer, H. L. Phillips.

Rocky Mountain Oil and Gas Association pioneers, 1953.
Sitting: C. S. Lavington, Denver; Warren Skelton, Casper; George Jarvis, Casper; A. E. Brainerd, Denver; Joseph Minton, Salt Lake City; A. J. Hardendorf, Lander; John Rouse, Denver; Edward J. Boos, Casper; James Donoghue, Denver; S. A. Lane, Garnett, Kansas. *Middle row:* Louis Hoffman (guest), Washington; H. C. Bretschneider, Denver; Charles J. Hares, Boulder; W. L. Connelly, Tulsa; T. S. Harrison (Moderator), Denver; E. J. Sullivan, Casper; C. B. Richardson, Casper; Warwick Downing, Denver; H. Leslie Parker (Moderator and President), Denver; Paul Stock, Cody; W. H. Ferguson, Denver. *Standing:* Earl Foster (guest), Interstate Oil Compact Commission; Frank Barrett (guest), U. S. Senator, Wyoming; Mr. Froyd (guest), Lusk (?), Wyoming; Ira Wetherill, Denver; Carleton Clymer, Denver; Martin Rathvon, Casper; George Jenkinson, Tulsa; H. A. Stewart, Washington; Dan B. Carroll, New Orleans; Robert Connaghan, Cheyenne; Mike Boyce, Casper; George Brimmer, Cheyenne; Frank Kistler, Glenwood Springs; Joe Juhan, Glenwood Springs; Harold Nutting, Denver; Harry Aurand, Denver.

pressed me as a man of ability. He expressed much interest in our work (as a matter of fact, he wanted us to find oil). We discussed the possibilities at some length, but the ultimate truth was to wait on our drilling operations.

A Mr. Vilhena, one of the Belgians interested in the concession, was at a diamond mine in the Congo. Capt. R. M. de Sarra Guedes, of the Angola Company, whom I had met in Lisbon, asked me to be sure and call on Vilhena and talk over our plans with him. In order to do this it was necessary for me to go into the northwestern part of Angola. I was glad of it because the trip afforded an opportunity to see the working of a diamond mine and to see more of the country.

A narrow-gauge railroad runs from Luanda to Malange, about 135 miles. Mr. and Mrs. Small accompanied me on the rail trip. The high commissioner and a party of officials were also aboard the train. As Malange is the end of the line, we arranged for a car to take us from that city to the mine, several hundred miles distant.

On our arrival at Malange, there was a celebration in honor of the commissioner. We were invited to attend, but for lack of time we had to decline, and we left about noon for the mines. We spent the night at Quintapa, where all three of us slept in the same room, which had a dirt floor and uncomfortable beds. For a change, the roads were fair! Many road gangs, consisting mostly of women, were working to put the roads in shape for the commissioner and his party, who were also headed for the mines.

We arrived at Saurimo at about 5 P.M. and were assigned to rooms in the diamond company's guest house. The governor of the province lived in this town, also several other white persons, mostly army officers and officers of the penitentiary located there.

We left early the next morning and arrived late that evening at Lunda, which was the post and headquarters of the

115

diamond company. The post guest house was filled, so we were quartered in the hospital. Colonel de Milo, the local military commander, gave a tea for us the afternoon of our arrival. We had dinner with Mr. and Mrs. S. T. Kelsey, Californians. Kelsey was superintendent of the mines. We had a pleasant evening.

After breakfast at Kelsey's, early the next morning, we drove about seventy-five miles to a diamond mine. Again the roads, built and maintained by the company, were good. Our first stop was at the pickup or sorting station. Here the gravel carts, sealed at the mine and containing gravel repeatedly screened, were opened by authorized officials, and the gravel was dumped onto the sorting tables. The workmen, all blacks, sorted the conglomerate and skillfully picked out the diamonds.

At the office we were shown about one thousand carats of uncut diamonds, which represented about two days' yield from the group of mines. Diamonds were worth about twelve dollars a carat uncut. Most of the stones from these mines made about one-fourth carat after being cut. The largest stone found up to the time of our visit was 54-carat.

From the sorting-rooms we went to one of the mines. The mining is a stripping process. About three feet of the soil is taken off by a steam shovel, exposing the gravel, which is dug into with a pick. The gravel is loaded onto a conveyor, which dumps it into a small car. The car carries the load to a series of screens. Silt is washed out; the coarser material is eliminated; and the remainder, about 10 per cent, is sent to the picking house.

On our way to the mine we passed a village where a *batuka,* or native dance, was in progress. We stopped to see it. A witch doctor, in fantastic garb, was doing a solo and putting all his enthusiasm into his job of turning, twisting, jumping, waving his arms, and yelling at the top of his voice. Other dancers formed a circle around the witch doctor and danced much like Indians in the United States. Music was produced with a home-made drum, which, though not of surpassing tonal quality, lacked nothing in point of booming penetration.

We had lunch with the local superintendent, a Belgian, and then returned to the main camp. While at the camp, I had a conference with Vilhena. He agreed with me as to the location of the new well and promised that on his return to Lisbon he would report favorably to the Portuguese and Belgian groups on our plan for drilling a well and would endeavor to have them raise their share of the money needed.

We left early the next morning on our return to Luanda, but did not make Xassengue until 10 o'clock that night. It was 11 before we got to bed. The rooms were hot and dirty. It was about 2 A.M., and we had scarcely fallen into a light sleep, when we were routed out of bed by three soldiers and taken to the commandant's office. There we were directed to show our passports. This was a highly irregular performance, but it was quickly apparent that the commandant had been imbibing something stronger than coffee. He had acquired delusions of grandeur and an ambition to impress foreigners with his transcendent importance.

Mrs. Small, who could speak Portuguese, made it clear to the commandant, in a few incisive words, that he had blundered. She showed him the high commissioner's safe-conduct letter. Her pointed little speech had an immediately sobering effect. The commandant dropped his imperious manner and offered abject apologies.

As soon as we were through breakfast we left Malange, and then drove to Donda, where we spent the night. This was our longest day's drive. We found our beds that night were well tenanted with vermin. We turned out at once and spent the rest of the night sitting up. David Livingstone, on his trip in the middle of the last century, took four months to get to

Luanda from Donda. Of course he had to cut trails and build rafts to ferry the rivers. It took us eight hours to make this trip from Donda and we were back in Luanda at noon of that day, after a trip of almost two thousand miles.

We did not see a horse or mule on the entire journey. All hauling was done by oxen. Strings of natives plodded along the roads, nearly all carrying five-gallon gasoline cans on their heads. Here was evidence I wanted to see, oil cans. Could we supply the demand locally?

I spent two days in the office at Luanda and then started for Boma, in the Belgian Congo, where I was to take a Belgian boat for Antwerp. On this trip, Small, Cranford, and I visited several oil seeps and some old wells that the Angola Company had drilled. We carried our camping outfit on a one-ton truck and camped the first night out near the town of Lefune. The next day we examined more seeps and camped that night at Onocula. Mosquitoes kept us busy, even though we had mosquito-bars over our cots. We got little rest. Besides Small and Cranford, two natives were with me as guides.

After another day of travel, we visited three old wells. No. 1 was still flowing oil and fresh water, making about three-fourths of a barrel of oil and about one-half barrel of water. There were no roads to the wells, the jungle having grown up since they had been drilled. We had to cut our own road. We had picked up a local guide at a village not far from the wells.

On our return to our camp we received a message from the chief of a tribe at the town of Macula, saying that a *batuka* would be given in honor of the "white chief from across the sea" (meaning me). The dance would start as soon as we arrived at the village. Many of the natives who had worked for the comany had lived here, and it was the home of one of the boys who was with us on the trip.

On our arrival at the village we were welcomed by the

118

chief. Through one of our black boys he said that his tribe was honored by my presence, and that he hoped I would give orders to put down some more holes in the ground so that his people would have much work. This was understandable since we paid 25 cents a day for labor as against 4½ cents by any other employer. After his speech and my reply, the *batuka* got under way. It was good but not as wild as the ones that we had seen in the interior. A boy of about seven years was the star.

We broke camp early the next morning and drove to Quelo to see another seep. This one was active and produced four quarts of a heavy black oil daily. There is no question that this country at one time would have produced oil, but it may have been thousands of years ago. We knew a good deal about the geology of Angola and parts of the Belgian Congo then, but we were subsequently to learn more. Much of Angola is underlain, at varying depths, by volcanic rock, which, if it does not mean that oil cannot be found there, at least limits the depth to which oilmen may go in search of pay.

But this was true of Osage County, Oklahoma, one of the richest oil pools in the nation a quarter of a century ago. Here much of the territory was underlain also by a great granite intrusion. At that depth and below it, no oil was likely ever to be found. Above it, at shallow levels, millions of barrels of oil were tapped, as I have shown in earlier chapters.

The twenty wells that the Angola Company, assisted by Sinclair, had drilled to shallow depths before I made my trip, were something like the oil seeps that had shown for hundreds, possibly thousands, of years. There just wasn't much oil present—certainly not enough to be considered commercially profitable. Now the question was, what might we get by going down deep—say five thousand feet (quite a depth for that time)?

This question was on our minds as we progressed slowly

119

to Quelo, to San Antonio Lazaire, and finally to Banana Point on the Congo, six miles wide here at its mouth, where I caught a steamer for Antwerp. Like the trip over, it was a slow, monotonous voyage, broken by the conversation of bored mortals like myself and by stops from time to time at ports of call.

In Brussels I conferred with the Belgian and Portuguese interests with whom we were joined in the Angola venture. We concluded that a "deep test" was in order at Cacoba Dome, which I thought of as the best possible location. Drilling operations there were subsequently got under way. We went down to 5,651 feet, where in 1930 we found a good but not paying limestone formation. This proved what the geologists knew, that the granite barrier was a good deal deeper; but it also proved that there was no oil at the most likely spot, at least not at our depth.

Sinclair and the Belgian and Portuguese interests controlling this concession in Angola some years later relinquished it. In 1953 Belgian drilling operations once more tried to find oil in commercially satisfactory quantities in Angola, in the same area we had chosen. But at 7,000 feet the pay dirt is not yet, nor is it ever likely to be.

I still don't like rough roads—unless they lead to oil.

11

MORE GLOBE-TROTTING

CALLED to the office of Harry Sinclair at about 5:30 o'clock one afternoon in early August, 1930, I received the surprising announcement that he and Mrs. Sinclair were to sail for Europe the next day and that he would like to have me take the trip with them. We would be gone about a month, he said. Harry sprang this news much as he might nonchalantly have suggested, "How about a bridge game this evening, Billy?" This was very much like the Russian jaunt in 1923.

"On what boat do we leave?" I asked as I tried mentally to list some of the swarm of details that would have to be taken care of in an extremely short time.

"I don't know," Harry responded. "Jack O'Day is making the arrangements. See him."

Jack was our traffic manager. I hurried to his office, only to find that he had gone for the day. It was 6 o'clock in the evening and I was to start the next day on an ocean voyage for which I had not made the smallest preparation. I didn't know the hour of the sailing. I didn't even know the name of the boat. I didn't have the money needed for an extended journey. (It was three months, instead of one, before we returned home.)

121

I next tried Earl Sinclair, who was able to provide much of the information I needed. Our boat, the *Aquitania*, would leave New York the following afternoon at 2 o'clock. That meant that I had less than twenty hours in which to snatch such sleep as I might and somehow attend to all the minutiae of preparation.

Having ascertained that our itinerary would make it possible, I thought that after reaching Europe it would be well for me to call on our partners in Belgium to discuss our affairs in Angola, Africa. Getting the data needed for such a conference kept me at my office late that night.

By dint of fast work, with a generous admixture of good luck, I was ready to sail when the time came. I had my passport in order, so there was no trouble on that score.

On the crossing to Cherbourg, France, where we were to land, I asked Harry why he had wanted me on the trip. "I'll tell you about that when we get to Paris," he replied.

At Cherbourg we were met by Harry Hassan with two automobiles. Sinclair and Hassan rode in one, Mrs. Sinclair and I in the other, and we were off for Paris. It was a delightful drive, giving us a much better view of the country traversed than would have been possible by rail. Our lunch at Bayeux, which Hassan had ordered in advance, was something to enjoy in retrospect long afterward. Here I had my first taste of Pont l'Évêque cheese, and I have been an addict ever since.

Mrs. Sinclair and I, both Catholics, wanted to pass through Lisieux, which had been the home of Ste Thérèse, the Little Flower. This we did, and we visited the church in which her body reposed. The casket was in a small room separated from the main body of the church by an iron grating. Through this grating the devout—as well as those not so devout—could pass any offering they desired to make toward the completion of a basilica in honor of the saint which was being erected on

122

a hill overlooking the city. When Harry saw these offerings, he inquired about them, and Mrs. Sinclair explained their purpose. Harry pulled out his purse and tossed in a one-hundred-dollar bill. (I did not wait to see whether the caretaker fainted when she picked it up.)

We arrived in Paris that evening after one of the most enjoyable auto drives I have ever taken. Jim Flanagan, an old friend from Tulsa, and his wife were in Paris, and having learned through the Paris edition of the *New York Herald* that Mr. and Mrs. Sinclair were in the city, they called on us. It was a happy reunion. While we were in Paris, Harry told me that he had brought me on the trip because he thought I had been working too steadily and needed a rest. (I have always smelled business on one of Harry's pleasure trips.) He said that we were going to Carlsbad for three weeks and that we would leave for that resort in a few days.

I decided that this was a good time for me to go to Brussels for the conference with our Belgian partners. Flanagan and I engaged a car and driver and drove to Brussels. Here we met Dick Gross, the treasurer of the Sinclair Company in Brussels. We spent three days in that city.

I made an appointment to meet our Belgian friends at their office at 11 A.M. one day. It was very hot and I arrived at the office in a profuse perspiration. The attendant at the office in which we were to meet was resplendent in full dress. Our Belgian friends were in morning attire and apparently were as hot as I was. The meeting was quite formal and prolonged. An appetizing luncheon served at the close of the meeting afforded some compensation for my discomfort. The conference was in other respects beneficial to both sides.

On our return to Paris we found that Mr. and Mrs. Sinclair, accompanied by Mr. and Mrs. Stacy Adams and Harry Hassan, had gone to Carlsbad. Adams was our company's manager for Belgium and Holland and was located in Brussels. I left Paris the next morning for Carlsbad, and on alighting from the train at that point I was greeted by Henry N. Greis, of Tulsa, who was on a European tour.

The party spent three weeks in Carlsbad. Before we left there Daniel T. Pierce, assistant to Sinclair, met us. The sale of the Sinclair half interest in the Sinclair Pipe Line Corporation and the Crude Oil Purchasing Company to the Standard Oil Company (Indiana) had been closed on the day he had sailed from New York. Earl Sinclair had handled all negotiations. The price paid was $73,000,000. We had previously sold a half interest to the Standard of Indiana.

This sale, while profitable enough in itself to the Sinclair companies, represented a move toward even larger goals on our part. We had already started thinking, indeed, negotiating, for the purchase of the Prairie Oil and Gas Company and the Prairie Pipe Line Company, which were then two of the largest oil properties in the Midcontinent area.

The oil business is like any other. When you can acquire large capital by a large sale, or if you can dispose of one operation and secure thereby an even better one, the rule is *sell!*

While in Carlsbad we were visited by Mr. and Mrs. Joseph Meyer, their daughter, and Karl Hasselmeyer, a geologist for Pettigrew and Meyer. Karl afterwards married Miss Meyer, and they now live in Houston. Karl is an officer in the Salt Dome Oil Company. Joe Meyer's visit was intended to interest Harry Sinclair in several thousand acres of leases that Meyer held in northern Germany.

While we were discussing this proposition, Meyer's Berlin office phoned him that a wildcat well drilling near Vienna, Austria, had come in as a large producer. Harry decided that we should take a look, so Joe, Karl, and I engaged an automobile and drove through Pilsen and Budweis (famous for you know what) and many other cities into Austria. We spent the first night at an inn just east of the border of Czechoslovakia. We had an early start the next morning and crossed the Danube shortly after dawn. Perhaps it was the Blue Danube Waltz that had led me to picture that stream as blue. It was anything but blue. It reminded me of the Arkansas River after a heavy rain.

It took us some time to find the well, but we finally got to it. The derrick was a stubby wooden affair about 48 feet in height, enclosed with a tight 16-foot board fence. Karl, of course, spoke German fluently, and after he had talked awhile with the watchman, who had worked on the well, we were permitted to enter the enclosure. The well was dead. It had made a spurt or two of oil and quit. Karl later made further investigations, but we dropped the idea of trying to find oil in Austria. After a night spent in Vienna we drove back to Carlsbad. We were glad we made the trip, if for no other reason than that it had given us an opportunity to view Vienna, a beautiful city rich in history.

At the conclusion of our stay in Carlsbad, Pierce left for Paris. The rest of us went by auto to Oberammergau and saw a performance of the Passion Play. Mrs. Sam Hildreth and Miss Gallagher, her niece, friends of Sinclair, joined us at Carlsbad and accompanied us to Oberammergau. The Passion Play made a deep impression on all of us. We went from there to Munich, where Pierce rejoined us. Mrs. Sinclair, Mrs. Hildreth, Miss Gallagher, and Mrs. Adams went to Paris.

Sinclair, Pierce, Hassan, Adams, and I left Munich by auto and drove along the Rhine River to Cologne. Leland Stanford, home director of foreign marketing, met us at Mainz and accompanied us to Cologne. The company's office for Germany was here, located in the Hoch Haus, tallest office building in Europe. After two days in Cologne we drove to Berlin. In Berlin we met Arthur Veatch, who until a few months before had been chief geologist for Sinclair's foreign work. We also met Chet Naramore, a one-time geologist for us, and Joe Meyer. This group had leases on thousands of acres in northern Germany and wanted Sinclair to take an interest in this acreage and to drill and develop it. We spent a few days considering this project but decided against it.

Mr. and Mrs. Adams left us in Berlin and returned to Brussels. The rest of the party went to Paris. Pierce left us in Paris and returned to New York. Sinclair had some business to attend to in Paris, where we spent three or four days. Then Mr. and Mrs. Sinclair, Hassan, and I, with Leland Stanford, who had joined us at Mainz, left for Rome, where Sinclair had an appointment to see Mussolini.

While we were in Rome it was our privilege to have a private interview with His Holiness Pope Pius XI. This was a great honor for all of us, but Mrs. Sinclair, Stanford, and I were probably more appreciative of its significance than any of the others. On this visit to Rome I met Count Enrico Galeazzi, with whom in later years I was to have much correspondence regarding affairs of the Order of the Holy Sepulchre. I was to meet the Count again in 1950 on a second visit to Rome.

Sinclair wanted to stop at Genoa on our way back to Paris, so we drove to the Port of Ostia, where we took an amphibian and flew to Genoa. It was my first airplane ride, and it afforded me a thrill. We maintained a height of seven or eight hundred feet, which allowed us a clear view of the country. Since this was a chartered plane, the pilot flew us over the island of Elba, where Napoleon had lived nine months in exile before he escaped to throw Europe into another war.

We left Genoa late the evening of the same day by rail for Paris, where we were met by a Herr Siefert, of the Gewerkschaft Elwerath. This company had oil production at Hanover and wanted to interest Sinclair in some kind of trade which would include our bulk plants and filling stations in Germany and the production of the German company. Together we were to build pipe lines and a refinery.

Sinclair viewed the proposition with some favor. After getting the groundwork for negotiations laid out, he left for New York. I stayed in Germany, at Hanover, and spent three weeks examining the leases and studying the daily production gauges. This was a task, as my knowledge of German was zero. I sent to Cologne for Ray Smith, who was in charge of our office there. He came to Hanover, bringing with him seven or eight young Germans. These lads I broke in as gaugers. The first few days' gauges were startling. Some wells apparently made hundreds of barrels a day, and some were making no oil at all. This strange state of things was soon remedied when we got the gauges in order.

While we were doing this work, I had made arrangements through P. W. Thirtle, comptroller of the Sinclair Consolidated Oil Corporation, to have Arthur Young and Company send auditors from Paris to Hanover and make an audit of the Elwerath books. After I had obtained this audit, and an audit of our books in Germany had been made for Elwerath, we started negotiations. These were carried on for several weeks with no results. During this time I had shipped to our Chicago refinery one thousand barrels of oil for analysis. We finally reached a deadlock in our negotiations, and after making arrangements for another meeting in New York in February, I returned home.

During my stay in Hanover I had been entertained at the house of a Herr Magnus, a banker and a director of the company with which we were dealing. Whether he was a descendant of Heinrich Gustav Magnus, the great German chemist of the nineteenth century, I do not know. His wife was English. During one of our conversations, Magnus said that he would like to have us take his eldest son into our company

127

and teach him the rudiments of the oil business. I promised to take up his request with Leland Stanford.

I talked the matter over with Leland on my return to New York, and the son later came to the United States. He first worked in some of the refineries, and later was transferred to the producing company working in the East Texas field. He was a bright chap, and undoubtedly would have made a good man for any oil company. He had been here for several months and had arranged to return to Germany when he was killed in an automobile accident at Troup, Texas.

When Hitler came into power, the Magnus family were exiled. After spending some time in Switzerland they started for the United States. They stopped in Cuba for a time. There Magnus met death in a motor accident in Havana.

The meeting set for February in New York was postponed and never did take place, so we did not enter Germany as a producing company. In view of the swift development of the second World War a decade later, this was probably a fortunate thing for us. German scientific genius coupled with determined exploration of the whole area of the Reich, excluding Austria, turned up in the years preceding the outbreak of war, a total of 4,074,000 barrels of oil annually. This was only .21 per cent of the world's total production, and by 1939, adding Austria's production to her own, Germany got only another 366,000 barrels a year—not enough to face up to the enormously greater production of the U.S.A., of 1,212,254,000 barrels, or of the U.S.S.R., 202,290,000 barrels. You simply can't fight wars without first possessing oceans of petroleum and the well-developed talents and facilities for processing these hydrocarbons into usable forms. And when it was said early in 1945 that "Japan is running out of gas," those of us in the oil business knew statistically what that meant.

But it would be a mistake to assume that, because no great oil structures have so far been located in Germany or Japan, no pools will be found in the future. I personally think great discoveries are unlikely—the geology of these countries tells us that—yet we have been known to find oil in the strangest places! In fact, we have in recent years drilled below earlier U.S. horizons where oil had been found, and down deep—six, eight, twelve thousand feet—we have found highly profitable pools. Also, in areas which seemed, from a geological point of view, highly doubtful, venturesome wildcatters have often made their bids and won.

E. DeGolyer, the well-known geologist and geophysicist of Dallas, Texas, is credited with a neat statement of the open-mindedness required in the search for minerals. At a recent meeting of scientists entrusted with stepping up the search for uranium, he suggested that the Navajos of New Mexico and Arizona be encouraged to join this effort. When pressed for his reason, he said, "Because in their search they will be wholly uninhibited by previous geological knowledge." He was subsequently proved right, for great new sources of uranium were discovered by these very Navajos, in one instance between strata of limestone, where, according to geology, they were supposed not to exist.

12

MERGER AND CONSOLIDATION

UNTIL ABOUT 1930 the Prairie Oil and Gas Company and the Prairie Pipe Line Company were dominant factors in oil in the Midcontinent area. The pipe-line company had been transporting crude oil through its several lines to Chicago, where some of it was delivered to the Standard Oil Company of Indiana, and the balance was put through trunk pipe lines that would deliver it to eastern refineries. It was a source of high revenue to the company. Some of its eastern customers were the Ohio Oil Company, Pure Oil Company, and Standard Oil Company of New Jersey. These companies endeavored to have the pipe-line company reduce its tariff, but they were unsuccessful.

These three companies, in 1930, organized the Ajax Pipe Line Company and built two ten-inch lines from Glenn Pool station in Oklahoma to Wood River, Illinois. Upon completion of these lines, the oil that Prairie had been transporting was diverted to Ajax. This took practically all of the Prairie Pipe Line's business from it.

The fact that the Sinclair Pipe Line Company had sold its pipe line to the Standard Oil Company of Indiana, which wanted to use the complete capacity of the lines for its refineries, thus depriving Sinclair of a way to move its oil to Chicago, was a windfall for the Prairie Pipe Line Company. Sinclair made a trade whereby the Sinclair oil would be transported through the Prairie pipe line. This kept Prairie in business. Sinclair had been working for some time on a trade whereby the Prairie Oil and Gas Company and the Prairie Pipe Line Company would be merged with the Sinclair Oil and Gas Company. When effected, this merger would give the Sinclair Company an outlet for the transportation of its oil to Chicago. These negotiations had been in progress over a period of several months. H. F. and E. W. Sinclair and Grattan Stanford, assisted by Dan Pierce, Joe Walsh, Reg Ragland, and many more members of our organization, put in days and nights working on the trade. Several times it appeared that an agreement had been reached, but the next meeting would bring up some objection. W. S. Fitzpatrick, Clark Kountz, Tom Flannelly, Dana H. Kelsey, Nelson Moody, and Fred Cook were the principals for the Prairie companies in the negotiations. But the merger was finally effected as of April 1, 1932.

The producing companies were merged under the name of Sinclair Prairie Oil Company, and the name of the Prairie Pipe Line Company was changed to Sinclair Prairie Pipe Line Company.

The Prairie Oil and Gas Company had a daily production of 31,467 barrels from 7,034 wells; the Producers and Refiners Corporation, 1,862 barrels from 284 wells; the Sinclair Oil and Gas Company, 32,055 barrels from 2,217 wells.

The producing offices were in Tulsa, and the pipe line company's were in Independence, Kansas. The officers of the Sinclair Prairie Oil Company were: W. L. Connelly, chairman of the board of directors; Henry L. Phillips, president; H. B. Smith, Dana H. Kelsey, W. W. Baker, H. A. King, vice presidents; A. E. Barrus, secretary-treasurer; Edward H. Chandler, general counsel; H. C. Fitzpatrick, assistant to the chairman of the board of directors.

The Sinclair Prairie Pipe Line Company's officers were: C. H. Kountz, chairman of the board of directors; J. R. Manion, president; Edward H. Chandler, vice president; R. B. Hanna, secretary-treasurer.

The Sinclair Prairie Oil Marketing Company was organized to purchase crude oil for the refinery requirements. The officers of this company were: Nelson K. Moody, president; E. B. Marlow and H. A. Meyer, vice presidents; A. B. Hookins, secretary-treasurer; Edward H. Chandler, general counsel. This company's offices were in Tulsa.

The name of the Sinclair Prairie Oil Company was changed on June 1, 1949, to Sinclair Oil and Gas Company. In December, 1950, the Sinclair Pipe Line Company was incorporated and all pipe lines, both crude and products, were transferred to it. Roy Tibbetts is chairman of the board and W. H. Morris, president, J. R. Manion having been retired.

As I had been elected an officer of the Sinclair Prairie Oil Company, it was necessary for me to transfer my residence from New York to Tulsa. This was done with pleasure for I was eager to be located in the heart of the producing fields.

In 1934 the Sinclair Prairie Oil Company purchased the J. A. Hull Company, with production in Oklahoma and Kansas, and since then it has made many other purchases of producing properties. As a result of these purchases, together with the drilling of wells and repressuring of old leases, the Sinclair Oil and Gas Company on May 1, 1952, had a daily net production of 112,897 barrels of crude and 7,080 barrels of natural gasoline. This production is steadily gaining each month, and with the increased drilling campaign, and the introduction of water-flooding (a recent engineering technique for increasing production of oil from old fields), it should soon amount to 150,000 barrels a day.

Recently H. B. Smith was made president, and J. W. Jordan executive vice president of the company. Mr. Smith's ability and the added authority given him, along with the splendid organization he heads, should make the production figure mentioned readily attainable before long.

As an officer of the Sinclair Prairie Oil Company I had, of necessity, many dealings with the legal department. Edward H. Chandler was general counsel. His first assistant was Ralph W. Garrett. Both are able attorneys, and they handled the manifold legal matters involved with dispatch. Chandler retired as general counsel in 1947, and Garrett succeeded him.

The merger caused some changes to be made in the personnel of the New York office. Sinclair still remained chairman of the board; W. S. Fitzpatrick became vice chairman; Herbert A. Gallagher, president; E. W. Sinclair was elected chairman of the executive committee.

A short two years after the Sinclair-Prairie merger, we began to acquire by purchase some additional valuable properties.

The Producers and Refiners Corporation was incorporated under the laws of Wyoming on May 14, 1917, with Frank Kistler as president and W. L. Kistler, vice president. The general offices were maintained in Denver.

Early in 1924, approximately 65 per cent of the outstanding capital stock of Producers and Refiners was acquired by the Prairie Oil and Gas Company. The offices were transferred to Independence, Kansas, on March 1, 1928. The Producers and Refiners had built a refinery and town at Parco, Wyoming, and had done considerable field development work. This construction and development had created a debt of $13,000,000. All of this amount became due and payable to the Prairie Oil and Gas Company.

Following the merger of the Sinclair Oil and Gas Company and the Prairie Oil and Gas Company into Sinclair

Prairie Oil Company, the indebtedness was assigned to the Sinclair Consolidated Oil Corporation. In May, 1923, L. R. Crawford and P. C. Spencer were appointed receivers for the Producers and Refiners Corporation. About 1926 Spencer was elected general counsel for Producers and Refiners, and Crawford was elected president. Spencer and Tom Johnson, of Wichita, Kansas, were appointed ancillary receivers for the state of Kansas, and Spencer and Crawford were appointed ancillary receivers for the state of Oklahoma.

In April, 1934, all the properties of Producers and Refiners were sold at receivership sales in the various states where they were located. Substantially all were purchased by the Sinclair Consolidated Oil Corporation.

R. W. (Reg) Ragland, assistant general counsel of the Sinclair Consolidated Oil Corporation, who was located in New York, came to Tulsa to arrange for the purchase of these properties. Herb Smith and I attended the sales in Oklahoma and purchased the refinery in West Tulsa and the producing properties in Oklahoma. I attended sales in Kansas, Wyoming, and Montana, and purchased the refinery, pipe lines, and producing properties located in those states. Reg accompanied me to these sales.

The purchases effected on these occasions have made the Sinclair Oil Corporation many millions of dollars and will continue to add more millions as the years go by. The Wertz Dome oil lease in Wyoming and the gas properties alone will reimburse Sinclair for the entire amount expended in all the purchases. Today these properties are worth many times the amount paid for them at the receivership sales.

Shortly after these sales had been completed, Spencer moved to New York as assistant general counsel of the Sinclair Oil Corporation. Ragland, in the meantime, had been transferred to Los Angeles as general counsel for the Richfield Oil Corporation, one-third of the stock of which was owned by Sinclair (the remaining shares being held, one-third by Cities Service, and one-third by the public). Crawford died in the latter part of 1934.

Money talked in these years, which formed the trough of the Great Depression. But from the evidence I have given earlier in this account it will be clear that, by sound over-all operations, the steady acquisition of good producing properties, pipe lines, and refineries, and, when desirable, the sale of properties for good, hard cash, the Sinclair Consolidated Oil Corporation was in good position to move forward even in difficult times. My own end of the business in the Sinclair Prairie Oil Company, consisting exclusively of production, contained the usual amount of Depression grief, however.

The big East Texas field came in as the 1930's dawned. The oil production that resulted was little less than a flood, and we were heavy producers there. About the time production reached its crest in East Texas, the Texas Company lowered the price of oil to 10 cents a barrel, which was obviously a good deal less than its cost at the well head. But that flurry didn't last long, fortunately. Through the efforts of many able men and organizations, proration, or the adjustment of production to demand, and stabilization gradually took shape. The determined work of Governor W. H. (Alfalfa Bill) Murray of Oklahoma, the Texas Railroad Commission, and the governors and corporation commissions and related agencies of the oil-producing states, deserve special recognition; and to Governor Murray's successor, E. W. Marland, goes credit for the creation in the mid-thirties of the Interstate Oil Compact Commission, which effectively controls the bulk of domestic production of oil in the United States.

By 1938, as the international situation hardened into a state of impending war, the oil industry was moving ahead in an orderly fashion. Oil was selling for a dollar a barrel, a price in line with its cost and pretty well adjusted to the needs of the consuming public at the time. We had weathered one of the worst catastrophes of American history—not without casualties, however, for the harsh requirements of the era had reduced payrolls, forced operating economies, and made more painful the risks we have always had to take in the oil business. But on the whole we fared as well as our previous foresight had entitled us to do, i.e. better than could possibly have been the case otherwise.

We were drilling deeper and getting engineering results that, in easier times, we might not have produced so swiftly. The great Oklahoma City field, which also got into operation in the early thirties, exemplified the new drilling ventures. Here we went down 6,500 feet and more with rotary drilling tools. The age of deep production was upon us. Now we think nothing of 12,000 feet, except when we total up the drilling costs and the dry holes. Costs are distinctly different today!

All through the thirties, we in Sinclair were searching for and getting new oil production. For it has to be remembered that producing wells are perishable commodities. Slowly and inevitably, despite the continuing engineering advances so necessary to our industry, oil wells decline in yield, until they give only a trickle like a cow going dry. Moreover, in these years oil remained what it was before, a highly essential product for the manifold operations of the motor car industry, air transport, railroads, buses, and truck lines—to name the obvious transport categories; and for all forms of industry, seaborne commerce, and the defense services. In other words, oil was still in relatively high demand even for the reduced industrial activity.

We were witnessing certain technological changes of great future importance to our industry and to the nation. Take the airplane, for example. Air transport during the depression years was greatly extended, planes were enormously improved, speeds and ranges were increased—and more and better motor fuels and lubricants were in demand. High octane gasoline began to be a factor of considerable importance in refinery operations.

Railroads were converting to Diesel motors, which require oil fuels rather than coal. In the homes of city folk, oil burners were coming into greater and greater use, again displacing coal for heating purposes. These are but samples of the trend which is continuing at accelerated pace today—greatly accelerated, because population is growing at a terrific rate.

I hate depressions for the reasons that everyone else hates them, but only more so: after all, I have sat in on more panics, recessions, flurries, and honest-to-God depressions than most people are likely to experience, for the reason that I've lived longer. But I sometimes get just the glimmer of hope in them. They seem to provide fertile ground for new ideas, new technical advances, new and radically different ways of doing things. It is only a curbstone opinion, but I'd guess we did some things in the oil industry during the ten years from 1930 to 1940 that we probably wouldn't have done in lusher times.

By 1939 we were producing in every oil state in the country, with the exception of California, where we were represented by Richfield, of whose stock we held, as I have said, one-third. As I have indicated, we had total production of well over 60,000 barrels a day, and we were processing all of it in our own refineries.

The opening of the new war in Europe in 1939 did to us what it did to all other essential lines—it put an immediate and heavy strain upon all of our departments. Then, as it became apparent that the United States would sooner or later become involved, the early pilot operations in Germany and over here for the production of synthetic rubber began to be of great practical significance. With our entry into the war, we were all forced into a war of many fronts in the petroleum field—high-octane fuels for aircraft; lubricants, fuels for

137

motor transport, tanks, and steamers and fighting ships; and now for synthetic rubber.

This is a very large story, with many technical by-paths, and it needs telling, but not here. What we succeeded in doing in the oil business was to make our existing steel and the reduced amount coming to us on allocation do a fantastic job. We were proud of personnel and of our industrial know-how, which produced the results required not by one nation but by half a dozen. In a war of movement, it was once more a demonstration of who got there fustest with the mostest. General Heinz Guderian was, by all accounts, a master tank tactician; but even German military genius falls away when fuel tanks are empty.

At Sinclair, we stepped up our total production to more than 85,000 barrels a day, and we processed a total much greater than that because of additional purchases. But this is in the refining department, and I've never had much to do with anything but production, where I feel entirely at home.

At the close of the war, the conversion back to peace-time activities required the better part of two years. But the demand for oil products in the domestic market skyrocketed the minute rationing of civilian demand was taken off. Since 1946, Sinclair has greatly extended its production, until today it approaches 150,000 barrels a day in countless old and new fields, and overseas. We have steadily increased our drilling activities, by the way, and water-flooding has contributed a surprising share of our increased production. This latter technical development is so remarkable that it merits at least a simple explanation.

Natural gas is the first lift in most newly opened fields. It is usually under great pressure in the underground trap where oil is found. As soon as this trap is penetrated by the drill bit, the normal consequence is for the natural gas to rush to the well head, carrying considerable quantities of crude oil with it. As time passes and gas pressure subsides, pumping operations are resorted to. These may continue for twenty, thirty, or forty years, depending upon the character of the oil sands, the rate of recovery of oil from them, and the relation of recovery costs to the price of oil.

Gradually the rate of daily production declines, however, and it would seem that the old pool has been exhausted. This is where water-flooding comes in. Engineers have found that a variety of repressuring methods can be employed—the forcing of natural gas back down into the oil sands, the use of compressed air, and the use of water under considerable pressure.

It just happens that most of the oil production of the United States lies in arid and semi-arid regions of the West. Hence we have had to overcome very large problems of water supply in effecting the water-flooding programs we have thus far undertaken. We get water from deep wells, by pipe lines from rivers, and from artificial catchments such as ponds and lakes made specifically for our purposes.

Joined with Phillips Petroleum Company and other companies, we have effectively water-flooded some 23,000 acres in the North Burbank field, which was badly played out after the war, twenty-five years after its discovery. The results have been highly satisfactory to everyone concerned, not least of all to the Osages, the royalty holders on all Osage County lands.

We have other properties under water-flooding operation, of course. The most recent transaction of importance that I had a part in was the purchase by the Sinclair Oil and Gas Company of the producing properties of C. C. Harmon, Howard J. Whitehill, J. Wood Glass, and others, for water-flooding. This was in August, 1951.

These properties were located in Nowata, Rogers, and Creek counties, Oklahoma. There were many leases and wells and nearly one thousand barrels daily oil production. The company's purpose was to obtain leases that were considered valuable for water-flooding. We already had a water-flood started on leases that adjoined some of those of Harmon, Whitehill, and Glass. Mostly these leases are located in the Delaware-Childers fields. The production is from the Bartlesville sand at a depth less than 750 feet. The sellers had some water-flooding under way, but since our acquisition of these leases, the production from them has largely increased.

Claude Harmon is an old-timer. He spent more than fifty years as a drilling contractor and producer and made it pay off. He was a Pennsylvanian and went to Kansas, making stops and working in West Virginia, Ohio, Indiana, and Illinois. He drilled the first well north of Cody's Bluff field, in Nowata County, in 1905.

Howard Whitehill is also from Pennsylvania. His father, Ben Whitehill, was one of the early-day successful producers in Nowata County. Claude and Howard had been associated for more than twenty years. I have been acquainted with both men for many years, and our association has been most pleasant.

As a matter of fact, water-flooding, like many another development in the oil business, came from my old stomping ground, Bradford, Pennsylvania. The Pennsylvania fields were the earliest commercially profitable operations in the United States. Hence the need for means of extending the recovery of oil from them prompted certain engineering thinking, which has since been of benefit to the entire industry. The pioneering efforts with water-flooding in the Bradford area began about forty-five years ago.

It has been estimated that the Bradford production has been increased more than 800 per cent by water-flooding since the time when increased recovery effects were first noted. While no doubt other, early floods were in existence, most of

140

them were operated more or less secretly and their results were not so obvious.

Even though water-flooding was started at an early date in Pennsylvania, it was not until the late 1920's and early 1930's that larger increases in production were obtained. In 1934 the first planned water-flood was started in Nowata County, Oklahoma. Here again there had been earlier haphazard operations in eastern Kansas and northeastern Oklahoma, but these had not produced the impressive results that were obtained with the pattern-flooding technique developed at Bradford. As a result of these developments, the water-flooding production in the United States increased from approximately 2,000,000 barrels a year in 1920 to approximately 20,000,000 barrels a year in 1937.

During the next decade there were spasmodic expansions of water-flooding activities into several new areas, but due to the distractions of the war effort together with the limited development supplies available, there were no big increases until from 1949 to 1950, when another large increase in water-flooding activities occurred. This most recent increase in activity has resulted in impressive gains in production in Kansas, Oklahoma and Texas. As an example, at the present time it is estimated that Oklahoma's water-flood production alone is more than the water-flood production for the United States in 1937. Kansas has also shown a large increase, and recent developments, particularly in west Texas, have indicated that large amounts of water-flood oil will be produced there also. With the prospects of still further expansions and applications in many fields and areas that are as yet untried for water-flooding, it is obvious that there will be much more oil produced by this process in the future.

As the present century approached the half-way mark, I was able not only to witness technical developments such as

141

I have described but to do some post mortems on projects that had been started many years before, either by the Sinclair companies or by me. One of these was the Venezuela survey, which, it will be recalled, occurred in 1929.

In April, 1946, Henry Phillips, while in Tulsa, told me Harry Sinclair had suggested that the next time Phillips went to Venezuela it might be advisable to have me go with him, that I had spent some time in that country and might have some ideas that would be of value. Henry said that he and Hugh Russell, a vice president of the Venezuelan Petroleum Corporation, expected to leave New York by plane on April 24 for La Guaira, Venezuela, by way of Miami, Florida, and suggested that I meet them there on the evening of that day. I did, and after a twelve-hour flight we arrived in La Guaira.

Ed Steiniger, our manager in Venezuela, met us at the airport and drove us to Caracas, where, during a four-day stay, I met many friends of my Venezuelan and Mexican days. Russell and I then left by plane for Barcelona. Kunhardt and Jim Evans, superintendent of the terminal at Porta La Cruz, met us at the airport. We drove to the port, where we spent the night. The next day Phillips and Steiniger joined us, and we drove over a good road (a surprise to me) to our camp at Santa Barbara. Dos Engle, who had been with the Sinclair Oil and Gas and Sinclair Prairie Oil companies as a district superintendent in Oklahoma, was in charge of drilling and lease operations in Venezuela. He spent the next four days taking me over the properties.

In the seventeen years since I had last been in Venezuela, much of value had happened to our properties. We had drilled both in the eastern interior, which is flat delta country, and in the west, which is mountainous. We had excellent production. It was clear to me that our earlier survey had been well worth the time and the jouncing on rough roads, and that our geologists and engineers had made no mistakes. As a matter of fact, at the time of the present writing, our total production in Venezuela amounts to about 18,000 barrels daily. There are now 4,000,000 shares of Venezuelan Petroleum Company stock in the hands of investors at about $26 a share.

Our royalty interest in the production at Lake Maracaibo has paid us handsomely all these years, over and above the production I note in the foregoing.

The Phillips Petroleum Company was drilling a well about three miles from our camp. On May 4, 1946, it was drilled in, but it got away from the crew and went wild. Kunhardt, Russell, Engle, and I spent the afternoon at this well. A wild well making one thousand barrels and many million feet of gas is a thrilling sight. There is always the danger that a fire may start, not so much the fault of the men working on the well as from the carelessness of spectators. Guards are stationed to keep outsiders at a safe distance, but in a jungle such as surrounded the Phillips well someone could easily get through the lines. I have seen wild wells catch fire and cause the loss of several lives. But fortunately this well was shut in after a couple of days of hard and dangerous work.

From Santa Barbara we drove to Barcelona, where we took a plane for Barranquilla, Colombia. Walter Wilson, our geologist in charge in Colombia, met us at the airport and we spent the afternoon in the office at Barranquilla. We took a car the next morning and spent most of the day driving over our concessions there. Then we drove into Cartagena, where we visited the old fort and other historical spots, flying back to Barranquilla in the evening.

On May 8 we left Barranquilla by plane for Miami, stopping at Jamaica and Cuba. Phillips and Russell flew back to New York, and I returned to Tulsa by plane through New Orleans. I can't think of a trip that was more profitable.

13

TIME EXPOSURE

IT IS IMPOSSIBLE to live with an industry, a faith, a way of
life for more than three-quarters of a century without being
impressed with progress. I know that this is a much over-
worked word in our language—the American language. But
the age of excitement is pretty well past for me, and I should
guess, without becoming dogmatic about it, that progress in
my time has been very real.

Carl Coke Rister, a very first-rate historian, has written
in detail and with accuracy and great interest the story of oil
developments in the Gulf Southwest from the beginnings in
1859 to the middle of our century.[1] I could not hope to do
what he has done in such a book, for mine is not a scientific
record but the impressions of a fairly active life. What I
know is that we began with no more motive power than you
could get from a human or a horse, and we have ended up
with everything but atomic power on the rig floor, at the
pumps, and in the pipe lines, refineries, and distributing arms
of the business.

The oil business has been, in a sense, self-generating.

[1] *Oil: Titan of the Southwest* (Norman, University of Oklahoma Press,
1949).

Without the combustible fractions developed in the refining process, we could not have had the internal combustion engine. Without the internal combustion engine, we would be far behind present-day operations, for that very engine is of primary importance in countless ways in the production of oil itself. Even so, we made progress for at least seventy-five years by means of the steam engine in drilling operations. Today we pump wells, for the most part, on an individual basis, with highly efficient stationary engines, using the products that we ourselves refine.

If an oil industry fair had been held around 1900, it would have been a sizable thing, counting all items required for the then existing operations. But there were no such fairs until 1923 when the first International Petroleum Exposition was held in Tulsa in April of that year. The show took place in the Convention Hall, a fairly large meeting place, to be sure, but it would never do for today's successors to that first effort. Now, thirty years after this particular kind of progress began, the show occupies twenty-eight acres along Twenty-first Street in Tulsa, with numerous large buildings to accommodate the exhibits. These exhibits cover almost everything used in the oil business, from a cotterpin to a rig capable of drilling twenty thousand feet deep. Only when you see this exposition can you appreciate the magnitude and the vast technical developments of the oil business of our time.

Visitors from forty-two countries were registered for the 1953 show, and close to 400,000 people attended. Here they could get first-hand information on, and demonstrations of, the methods and technical devices which have greatly facilitated operations since we began with more primitive equipment during my early years in oil: rotary bits of infinite hardness, geophysical instruments, special muds used for rotary drilling operations, high-pressure lubrication systems, and an innumerable lot of devices, most of them newly developed, for achieving with precision what we fumbled for in the beginning years.

My hat is off to the engineers and the pure scientists. What they have done to transform our industry is clearly evident to us all. They have done everything but remove the risk of dry holes, which remain—and will always remain—the sobering hazard of our enterprise. When I think of these contributions, I feel not a little humble. For such men and others, notably executives from the industry, have honored some of us old-timers much beyond our deserts. Following is the list of those who received gold medals at the 1953 International Petroleum Exposition:

Pioneer of Pioneers—Harry J. Crawford, Emlenton, Pennsylvania, chairman of the Board of Quaker Oil Refining Company, with sixty-five years of service and an impressive record of achievement.

Transportation—Wallace R. Finney, Scarsdale, New York, former head of all pipe lines for Standard Oil Company of New Jersey.

Natural Gas—Godfrey L. Cabot, Boston, Massachusetts, president, Godfrey L. Cabot, Inc.; ninety-two years old and still active.

Refining—Edwin B. Reeser, Tulsa, retired in 1943 as president of Barnsdall Oil Company; past president of American Petroleum Institute, with distinguished service in many fields of oil.

Natural Gasoline—George G. Oberfell, Bartlesville, former vice president of Phillips Petroleum Company and now vice president for research and development of American Chemical Society.

Supplies and Equipment—Wallace D. Wilson, Houston, president of Wilson Supply Company, with over forty years of service in the supply business.

Production—W. L. Connelly, Tulsa.

Mrs. Connelly and I on our fiftieth wedding anniversary.

Wet, bone tired, but happy.   The best walk a man ever took.

The wilderness is still very productive.

P. C. Lauinger, publisher of the *Oil and Gas Journal,* was master of ceremonies and the exercises attending presentation of the medals. W. G. Skelly, president of the Skelly Oil Company, made the presentations. A medal was awarded Miss Ernestine Adams, of Dallas, as the outstanding woman of the oil industry. It was presented by W. K. Warren, chairman of the board of Warren Petroleum Corporation. It was the first time such an award had been made. B. L. Majewski, president of the Great American Oil Company, Chicago, was the principal speaker.

There is no denying the fact—as I made clear early in this book—that I was married first to the oil business and only several years later to my wife. If anyone made a splendid partner in the scrambled, hurried, haphazard life which the oil business exacts, she was that one. Her devotion to me and my business affairs—New York, Europe, Mexico, Venezuela, Angola (if I could only forget those rough roads!)—is the stuff of which saints are made.

On October 4, 1948, Mrs. Connelly and I had been married fifty years. Our daughter and son, Elizabeth and Harry, decided that it would be nice to have a celebration for us on our golden wedding anniversary. A good friend, Bishop Eugene J. McGuinness, of Oklahoma City, gladly consented to attend the celebration and say a pontifical high mass. The mass was celebrated in Christ the King Church, Tulsa. There must have been at least five hundred of our friends present. Later a luncheon was given at the Tulsa Club.

Among those present at both the mass and the luncheon were two persons who had been present at our marriage, my brother, E. J. Connelly, of Oklahoma City, and J. J. Cooney, of Toledo. At the luncheon the Bishop read a cablegram from the Vatican bestowing on Mrs. Connelly and me the papal blessing and conferring on Mrs. Connelly the honor of Lady of the Order of the Holy Sepulchre.

She was to enjoy half a dozen more years of life, until the summer of 1954, when she passed away.

It becomes pretty easy, after you pass seventy, to tell other people how to live. In fact, it's a kind of perpetual temptation, apparently. Up to this point I have resisted it stoutly. But now that I must account in print to the younger generations, I may as well state a few convictions.

Simple piety is something we can all seek, with spiritual and moral profit to ourselves and our contemporaries. Attaining it is the work of two lifetimes.

Religious and racial tolerance have made more genuine progress since my boyhood than any of us born in the last quarter of the nineteenth century could have thought possible.

To assist people of every faith to their own fulfillment has always seemed to me a first order of business.

To say that one has received great benefits from his church is to risk the obvious, self-directed question, "How much did you put into it?" The answer is, "Not enough." Be that as it may, Pope Pius XI, with whom I had had a private audience on my first visit to Rome, accorded me, in 1933, the decoration of Knighthood in the Equestrian Order of the Holy Sepulchre of Jerusalem. In 1935 I was advanced to Knight Commander and on May 3, 1937, to the rank of Grand Cross. I became at that time president of the Western Lieutenancy of this order in the United States. Later I became lieutenant, and after a second term was succeeded by P. C. Lauinger of Tulsa.

In 1950, with Mr. and Mrs. William J. Sherry, I made the Holy Year Pilgrimage to Rome. Mrs. Connelly had planned to go, and we had delayed our departure in the hope that she would be able to do so, but in the end she did not feel strong enough. In Rome we were able to witness all of those solemn and impressive ceremonies which were in progress during our stay there. Moreover, we were received in private audience by the Pope. In excellent English he stated that he was delighted that so many Americans had made the pilgrimage, and that he was a sincere admirer of the United States and had once visited us (shortly before his election to the Papacy). On being told, in answer to a question, that we were from Oklahoma, he remarked, "An oil state." He conversed with us for about ten minutes, gave us each a Holy Year medal, and bestowed his blessing upon our families and our business. For all his seventy-five years, he was active and alert. Our private and public audiences inspired a feeling of reverence which will always endure.

There remains a conviction about which I have no reticence, qualms, or restraint. I am firmly convinced that the average person doesn't get in half enough fishing during a lifetime. If I had my life to live over again, I would join a movement, pay fees, and do anything else necessary to see that all men (and women) got the opportunity, at least, to fish often. And in this I subscribe to an often-repeated criticism directed at us by people from abroad: that we don't know how to relax. That's right. We don't. And that includes me.

In the time I have been able to give it, I have had immense enjoyment from fishing in waters from Canada to South America. But the friendships I have made in this pleasant diversion have given me the greatest pleasure of all—people like Scotty Petty, Horace Fitzpatrick, E. E. Kirkpatrick, Mr. and Mrs. Hal C. Price, Jack Jordan, Dana Kelsey, Jim and Kathrine Gallagher, Herb Rhees, the Sherrys—I can't name them all (maybe I got in more fishing trips than I thought).

One unforgettable fishing expedition was on a yacht owned by Erle P. Halliburton, president of the Halliburton Oil Well Cementing Company, named the *Vida*, in honor of his wife. It was a beautifully appointed boat in every detail, 236 feet long, 34-foot beam, 14 feet of draught, and powered with two 1,100-horse-power diesel engines. Erle bought the boat principally for the use of his gold mining company in Honduras,

149

but he decided to entertain some of his friends before putting it into that service. Several hundred were his guests on moonlight cruises during the week of the oil show in 1935 in Houston, and a few weeks later Claude P. Parsons, a top executive of the Halliburton Company invited thirty-two representatives of Midcontinent oil companies to take a fishing trip on the *Vida.*

The party, which was to assemble at Port Aransas, Texas, included Harry Weiss, John Suman, and Jim Anderson, of the Humble Oil Company; Ray Kelly and Ken Covel, of Pure Oil; and representatives of other companies. Claude had told me to bring six or seven Sinclair men with me. I asked Paul McDermott, Dana Kelsey, Fred Cook, Nelson Moody, and Horace Fitzpatrick.

On Friday, May 26, 1935, we put out from Aransas Pass. It was a beautiful evening. We had a most delicious dinner, with all that would make it enjoyable. We headed for the Eighth Pass, in Mexican waters, intending to enter the pass, anchor in deep water, and fish from small boats; but our plan had to be changed, as the *Vida* drew too much water to cross the bar. It was decided to lower the launches from the *Vida* and cross the bar in them.

The first boat lowered took off several fishermen without mishap. The second, of which I was an occupant, was beset by trouble from the start. The sea was high, and the boats bobbed up and down on the swells. As Fred Cook stepped from the stairway, the boat took a sudden drop and he landed in the Gulf. He was pulled out wet but unhurt, save for ruffled dignity. Fred was urged to change his clothes, but he loftily refused. It was warm and his clothes would soon dry, he said. So across the bar we went.

We had gone only a short way into the pass when our engine stopped. With all that oil-field talent aboard, we should

150

have been able to make repairs, but some small gadget was broken and we just rolled around on the sea.

The first boat was now about two miles from us, and as its occupants were catching fish, they paid no attention to our plight. The third boat soon entered the pass, however, and it came to our assistance. An engineer on it boarded our boat. He could do nothing with the broken part, so he put all the passengers from his boat into ours and started back to the *Vida* for repair parts. Our overloaded boat was so crowded that we had no room to fish.

The engineer's boat broke down before he reached the yacht, and there was no other boat to get men or parts to us. Finally Boat No. 1 came to our help and took some of our passengers into it. We then had room to do some fishing. And it was good fishing. The first boat stayed fairly close, so that it could tow us if we wanted to move.

The sea began to get rougher, and it was agreed that it would be best for all of us to return to the *Vida*. Boat No. 1 hooked onto us, and we started for home. Then No. 1 developed trouble, with the result that both boats were helpless. Soon a shrimp boat came along, hooked onto both our boats, and again we were on our way. It was now getting dark, and we were all drenched by the waves breaking over us. When we reached the bar, the sea was so high that the shrimper would not attempt to pull us over it.

Our party disembarked on a sand bar, which we named "Mosquito Point" in recognition of its principal attraction as a vacation spot. Here we spent the night. No food, no beds, no cigars, and all wet to the skin. We could look across the water about two miles and see the *Vida*, all lighted up and dancing on the waves. It was easy to imagine what kind of time those on board were having. Most of us scraped out hollows in the sand, lay down in them, and got what sleep the mosquitoes would allow. So the night passed. Those who didn't try to sleep did some fishing.

Early in the morning the boat that had gone in for repair parts appeared at our ocean resort and took us to the *Vida,* where we put in some heavy work at the breakfast table.

While we had been marooned, things were happening at the *Vida.* The boat in which Nels Moody rode had remained in the Gulf proper to fish there. When the waves became violent it returned to the *Vida.* By this time the Gulf was so fierce that it was not safe to bring the launch close enough to the yacht to transfer the fishermen. A boom and rope ladder were used to unload the launch. Several of the men negotiated the ladder safely, but Nels Moody, after catching the lowest rung, could not raise himself for a foothold. While he was dangling and the boatman was maneuvering to get the boat under him, T. L. Lewis, of Houston, fell overboard from the launch. All hands yelled, "Man overboard!" Then Moody lost his hold on the ladder, and he too slipped into the water.

There was great commotion, with all hands trying to help in a rescue. The two men managed to get a hold on the launch, but attempts to haul them into it were unsuccessful. A sailor finally dived from the *Vida* and got a life preserver on Moody. A rope had been tied to the preserver, and with some of the men in the launch pulling on the rope and others grabbing Moody's arms, belt, or shirt, the floundering man at last was hauled into the launch. Soon afterward Lewis was drawn in.

All this time the waves were shooting the launch into the air one moment and sinking it in the sea the next. Both Moody and Lewis were exhausted, and it was at least an hour before they were able to board the *Vida.* In the meantime they had a bobbing session on the waves. In a couple of hours they had fully recovered from any ill effects. Of course, we who were marooned on Mosquito Point knew nothing of all this excitement until we returned to the *Vida* in the morning.

All of this was, however, but the adventurous prelude to a terrific fishing success which followed. We caught fish of many varieties, on bait, on lures, by trolling, and with hooks set to run deep. Many forces of nature have conspired to make this area one of the great fishing spots of the world.

14

THE BIG BRASS

I CANNOT CONCLUDE this book without some notes on Harry Ford Sinclair and other men I have known in the oil business. I have been associated with many of the great and near great in the oil game. Some of these men were intimate friends and some were business acquaintances; but Harry Sinclair, to my mind, has a quality of distinction all his own. I know no other of his caliber. He is the only one of his model. He apes no one but stands on his own platform. He has always fought for what he considered right, even if he fought alone. He built a mighty oil empire. I know of no other man who could have done quite the job he did. Countless difficulties and obstacles arose to hinder and harass him, but his determination and supreme faith in himself carried him to his goal, to found a great oil company.

During many of his really dark days he was surrounded by only a handful of sincere friends, but he never lost faith in himself. In half a century he has put the Sinclair name in every state of the Union (in the Far West through the Richfield Oil Corporation). Almost single-handed he won the fight against the Anglo-American Oil treaty. He is a man of tremendous drive and energy and expects these attributes from his associates. He has never wheedled or coddled. He gave orders and expected them to be executed, but when he gave his friendship it stuck as long as it was deserved.

Sinclair is exceedingly charitable. Many individuals, churches, and organizations have been the recipients of his generosity. I remember an amusing incident in this connection. While his offices were in Tulsa he received a letter from a widow who lived some place in Kansas, telling him that her cow had died, that she had no money to purchase another, and that she needed milk daily for her children. She asked him if he would send her the money to purchase another cow. He sent her a check that in those days would have bought two or three cows. The widow acknowledge his gift in a nice letter and said that the only way that she could show her gratitude was to name the cow Harriet. H. F. got a great kick out of this.

Many members of the Sinclair Oil Corporation have received a helping hand from H. F. when the going was rough for them. I have been with him for nearly fifty years, from the time when his office consisted of three rooms over the old post office in Independence. I have spent a great deal of time with him in driving over oil leases, first in buckboards and then in autos; in the office, on trains and ships, and on European trips. I believe that I know him.

He can be kindly and considerate or as tough as a Kansas cyclone. He is taking life easier in these days, but I am sure that he would prefer being out on the firing line as he was thirty-five or forty years ago. If he could do this I would want to be with him. In May, 1954, he retired from the Board of Directors of the Sinclair Oil Corporation, but he remains honorary chairman of it. As long as the organization he built bears his name, Harry Sinclair will continue to breathe and think and dream oil. For it is the stuff by which he—and all of us who were associated with him—made an impression upon the industrial structure of America and forwarded the development of the world.

155

Earl W. Sinclair died on September 21, 1944. His death was a blow to the corporation. He was one of the most likable of men. His temperament was entirely different from that of his brother Harry, and he was a balance-wheel during many of our difficult days. His death, a distinct misfortune to Harry, was felt keenly by all of us, and I always feel his absence when I visit the New York office. I think that the death of Earl Sinclair hit all of the organization harder than that of any other person.

Percy Craig Spencer, who now heads the Sinclair Oil Corporation as president, was born in 1893 in Jasper, N.Y. In 1903 his family moved to Cody, Wyo. He may well be called a Wyomingite. After graduating from high school, he attended the University of Nebraska. In 1912 he returned to Cody as editor of the *Cody Enterprise*. Later he completed work in the Law School at the University of Nebraska and received his degree. He joined the army in 1918 and on discharge became secretary to United States Senator Francis E. Warren of Wyoming. In 1922 he was made executive secretary of the Wyoming Republican State Committee. Two years later, when Judge T. Blake Kennedy retired as chairman of the committee, Spencer was chosen to succeed him.

I have already explained his entry into the Sinclair organization, on the purchase of Producers and Refiners Company in 1934. Serving first as assistant general counsel, he was advanced to general counsel, executive vice president, then president. In June, 1949, he received the degree of LL.D. from the University of Wyoming. A number of us from the Sinclair organization had the pleasure of attending this ceremony.

I would not detract one iota from the wonderful work performed by Harry Sinclair in thirty years of organizing and building the Sinclair Oil Corporation and guiding it to its high place in the industrial world. No one but Harry could have done this. But "Spence" is the man most qualified to build upon these solid foundations. He has farseeing vision, and his executive ability is of the highest order. He is unceasingly at work on new programs for the progress of his corporation. He is understanding and considerate in his dealings with subordinates, who give him their best not because he is boss but because he enjoys their unqualified good will. His standing in the oil industry, moreover, is surpassed by no other person.

Sinclair made a discerning choice in the selection of his successor. Under Spence's guiding hand the Sinclair organization cannot be stopped by anything short of a calamity.

I know the warmth of this man's personal friendship, which is returned in the fullest degree. Owing to my advanced years I cannot hope to give him the active help I would like, but I never shall forget his kindnesses.

I first met another of today's top executives, Marvin Gosney, at a meeting in Chicago. Fletcher Farrell gave a luncheon for Harry Sinclair and some of us who were on an inspection trip. Marvin was among those present. He was a nice looking boy of about 23 or 24 years, with pink cheeks and a rather quiet manner. After he had been with the organization a short time he shed his retiring disposition. He came into the Sinclair Refining Company, which at that time had its principal offices in Chicago, through Farrell. Both had been with the Fort Dearborn National Bank.

Farrell was at this time treasurer of the Sinclair Refining Company. Marvin was made his assistant. Later Earl Sinclair resigned as treasurer of the holding corporation, and Farrell was elected to that office, moving to New York and taking Marvin with him as assistant treasurer. On Farrell's death, Marvin was elevated to the treasurership of the Sinclair Consolidated Oil Corporation. He had worked with Farrell so long that there was no interruption of any of the treasury activities. He handled all of the thousand and one things that would come up day by day in such a large organization. All of the treasurers of subsidiary companies reported to him, asking his advice on matters that perplexed them.

On Harry Sinclair's retirement as president of the corporation, Spencer was elevated to that office, and Marvin became, through merit, the executive vice president. In this position he has become Spencer's right-hand man. He is widely known among bankers. He is a tireless worker, and takes home with him evenings enough work to keep him busy until night, but he is one of the first on the job in the morning. Whenever he can get away from it all for awhile, he goes fishing, and according to his companions on those trips, he catches what he goes after.

On May 26, 1952, he received an LL.D. from the University of Tulsa, a well-deserved recognition. He is understanding and agreeable, but, when the occasion demands, he can be as hard-boiled as anybody. He probably has retained his youthful appearance to a greater degree than any other person in the corporation.

It was in Peru, Kansas, back in 1903 or 1904 that I first met a man whose name has appeared often in my account. Al Watts was destined to fill a major role in the Sinclair companies. At that time he was in charge of a store for the Oil Well Supply Company. He remained with that company until January, 1916, when he came into the Sinclair organization. When the Sinclair Oil and Refining Corporation was organized in May, 1916, Watts was made an officer and director, and he moved to New York. He has had charge of many of the corporation's subsidiaries during the thirty-five years that have elapsed since then. He was in charge of the Sinclair Navigation Corporation, the Sinclair Cuba Oil Company, Freeport Mexican Oil Corporation, Mexican-Sinclair Oil Corporation, and many other subsidiary companies. He has been a factor in advancing the corporation to its high position among leading corporations of the country. He is at the present time a vice president and director of the Sinclair Oil Corporation.

In June, 1916, Henry L. Phillips came to me at the office of the Sinclair Pipe Line Company, in Tulsa, to see if there might be an opening for him in the organization. He had graduated in law at Ohio State University, had been admitted to the Tulsa County Bar, and was employed by Charles Page, the oil producer, industrialist, and philanthropist of Sand Springs.

I introduced Henry to Ed Chandler, the head of our legal department, and it was arranged that the young man should enter the Sinclair Pipe Line Company service on July 1. Henry spent some time there and then was moved into the Sinclair Crude Oil Purchasing Company as president. From there he went to the Sinclair Oil and Gas Company as president. At the time of the merger with Prairie, the Sinclair Oil and Gas Company name was changed to Sinclair Prairie Oil Company, and later to Sinclair Oil and Gas Company.

Henry moved into the New York office in 1941 as the New York contact for all producing and pipe-line matters. He is now chairman of the Board of Directors of Sinclair Oil and Gas Company. In addition, he is a vice president and director of the Sinclair Oil Corporation and a director of the National Bank of Tulsa.

As New York representative of the oil company, Henry has been a tower of strength to the operating forces, not only in Tulsa but wherever located. He served for years as board chairman of the Venezuelan Petroleum Corporation.

Besides the men already mentioned, I am indebted to many others in the New York office for warm good will manifested throughout the many years of the Sinclair companies' existence. I cannot enumerate all of them here, but I would be derelict if I failed to mention Joseph P. Walsh, general counsel, who repeatedly has gone out of his way to extend kindly offices to me and members of my family. And how can I refrain from naming such good friends as Byrne McDonald, Sheldon Clark, Fred Bush, Hugh Russell, Percy Thirtle, Charley Allen, and W. F. Dau? Among my treasured memories are those of pleasant hours spent with all.

During my years as a company officer in Tulsa I came to know and esteem hundreds of the men and women who were giving their best efforts to Sinclair growth and expansion and to the varied tasks assigned them. For their loyal support I owe more than I ever can repay. I am sorry that all their names cannot be given here. It would mean listing virtually all the names on the payroll.

There are two whom I should especially mention. During my entire business career I have had but two secretaries. They perhaps can say whether I am hard to get along with. Miss Margaret Dougherty filled the position from November, 1912, until March 15, 1934. She moved with us to Houston in 1917, to Casper in 1922, to New York in 1928, and back to Tulsa in 1932. In 1934 she resigned and was married to J. E. Rocheford. She now lives in Oakland, Calif. Mrs. J. E. (Margaret) Patterson was one of the staff of the Sinclair Exploration Company in New York. When I moved there she assisted Miss Dougherty in some of the latter's duties, and on Miss Dougherty's resignation I asked Mrs. Patterson to take Miss Dougherty's place. Accordingly she came to Tulsa and after twenty years is still with me.

This suggests that I am still at work. As a matter of fact, I am, even though I retired from active participation in oil affairs on January 31, 1950, my seventy-seventh birthday, when I resigned the chairmanship of the Board of Directors of the Sinclair Oil and Gas Company. There are still a good many odd jobs for a man of eighty-one to do, and having a reasonably strong heart, I still find the doing of them zestful. The pursuit of any goal, it seems to me, stops short only at oblivion. One never has enough of what one is after, which, as the after-dinner speaker is wont to remark, reminds me of a couple of stories.

Gunsberg and Foreman were large producers in Oklahoma around 1908 and for many years afterward. They had a lease near Delaware in which Paul Lovell owned an interest. Driving past this lease one morning, I noticed that workers there were about to shoot a well.

In those days we shot a well "open," with the result that a great mass of fluid, mixed with sand, would be blown into the air forty to one hundred feet above the top of the mast on a Star drilling rig. It was a stirring sight and I never failed to get a thrill out of it. Johnny Larkin and Ernest Connelly, who then owned the Eastern Torpedo Company and now own the Larkin Torpedo Company, burned up thousands of quarts of nitroglycerin each month in these shooting operations.

I was well repaid for stopping to see this particular well shot. It was a magnificent spectacle, and when the well started flowing, it was apparent that it was good for five hundred to seven hundred barrels a day.

Davy Gunsberg was at the well, but Paul was not. I turned to Davy and congratulated him on his nice well.

"My God!" he exclaimed. "That Paul Lovell is a lucky man!"

Gunsberg and Foreman owned seven-eighths interest in the well, and Paul one-eighth!

This insatiable drive for more barrels is illustrated also in the story of the oilman's heaven.

An oilman died and appeared at the pearly gates for disposition of his case.

"Your name and occupation?" asked Saint Peter.

"I was an oilman," the newcomer told him.

After consulting his book, Saint Peter announced: "You are entitled to enter, but we have had such an influx of oilmen recently that the quarters provided for them are overcrowded. We are building additions, but it will be a few days before they are ready. Just rest outside the gates, with the assurance that you will be taken care of soon."

The oilman considered the situation for a moment and then came up with an idea (he must have been a Sinclair landman). "If you'll let me have ten minutes with your oilmen," he said, "I'll guarantee that you'll have plenty of room. You won't need any additions."

"Highly irregular," returned Saint Peter. "However, your proposition sounds good to me. But only ten minutes, mind you. Not a second more." Then, calling an angel, he directed, "Take this man to the oilman's section. Keep your eye on him, and have him back here in ten minutes."

Five minutes later the heavenly calm was shattered by a stampede of oilmen, shouting excitedly. "Open the gates! Let us out!"

The startled Saint Peter unlocked the gates. In amazement he watched the disorganized stream of oilmen race headlong to the edge of the celestial precincts, where they leaped off. As the commotion died out, the angel and his charge reappeared.

"What happened?" demanded Saint Peter, as he stooped to recover a bunch of keys which had slipped from his hand in the excitement. "In all the centuries that I have been here nothing like this ever happened."

"Well," grinned the oilman, "I walked over to a crowd of fellows who were swapping stories about boom oil towns, and I said, 'Hello, boys! I have news for you. A 10,000-barrel wildcat well has just been drilled in at 4,000 feet!' 'Where?' they yelled. 'In Hell,' I answered. 'Leases are available.' And the rush was on."

With St. Peter's tacit approval, the oilman returned to the now unoccupied oilmen's section of Heaven. But it proved to be a very lonesome place. No one to talk to. No one to talk about. No reminiscing about Burkburnett, Whizbang, El Dorado, Bowlegs, Tampico, East Texas, Glenn Pool, Louisiana, Oklahoma City. Was this really Heaven?

Approaching St. Peter again, this time cautiously, the oilman asked if the great gates could be opened for him.

"Why do you ask this?" said St. Peter.

"I have been thinking," said the oilman, "about that rumor of oil in Hell. There might be something to it."

APPENDIX

W. L. Connelly's First Oil Lease

<table>
<tr><td>G. H. HARMAN & W. H. WHITMAN
TO
WILLIAM L. CONNELLY</td><td>This agreement Made and entered into this 21 day of February A.D. 1895 by and be-tween G. H. Harman</td></tr>
</table>

and W. H. Whitman of the County of Wood and State of Ohio of the first part and William L. Connelly of Toledo, O. of the second part. Witnesseth That the said party of the first part for and in consideration of the agreement herein after men-tioned, has granted demised and let unto the party of the sec-ond part for the purpose and with the exclusive right of drill-ing and operating for petroleum and gas all that certain tract of land situated in Portage Township Wood County and State of Ohio being in Section Number 23 said Township and bounded and described as follows to wit: The East half (½) of the East half (½) of the North half (½) of the South West quarter less one half (½) acre out of the North East Corner and The West half (½) of the North West quarter (¼) of the South East quarter (¼) of said section twenty three Township four (4) North of Range Eleven East Con-

165

taining thirty nine & one half (39½) acres be the same more or less. Together with the right of way over said premises to the place of operating the right to lay pipes to convey water oil and gas, and the right to remove any machinery or fixtures placed on said premises by the party of the second part. The party of the second part are to have and to hold the said premises for and during the term of five years from the date hereof and as much longer as oil or gas is found in paying quantities. The said first party shall fully use and enjoy said premises for farming purposes, except such parts as may be necessary for said operations and no well shall occupy more than one acre. In Consideration of said grant and demise the said party of the second part agree to give or pay to the said party of the first part the full equal one sixth (⅙) part of all oil produced or saved from the premises and to deliver the said free of expense into tanks or pipe lines to the credit of the first party and should gas be found in sufficient quantities to justify marketing the same the consideration in full to the party of the first part shall be $200\,^{00}\!/_{100}$ per annum for the gas from each well so long as it shall be sold therefrom and gas free of cost for household use on the premises also from oil wells for two stoves. It is agreed that there shall be no wells drilled within three hundred feet of the buildings now on the premises with out consent of the first party. It is further agreed that the party of the second part shall complete three wells on the above described premises by the 1st day of June 1895 unavoidable delays excepted or in default thereof to pay to the party of the first part three hundred dollars. It is fully understood by and between the parties hereto, that the rights and privileges herein conferred shall be construed to mean simply a lease of privilege to drill and operate as above set forth for gas and oil and any attempt on the part of the second party to exceed the privileges granted as so construed shall render the same liable for trespas and furthermore shall

166

work a forfeiture of all rights conferred, and this instrument shall become null and void. Second party is to have the right to use gas, oil or water for operating but not for drilling and further second party agrees to drill and complete six wells on said land in manner following to wit first three as above stated and one well each successive sixty days thereafter until all are completed. Should second party fail to comply with or surrender this lease each well drilled thereon shall retain six acres surrounding it. Also the second party is to deposit $300 $^{00}/_{100}$ to the credit of the first party in Ketcham's Na Bank of Toledo, O. for the faithful performance of this contract if he should fail to drill the first three wells it is forfeited to first party when first three wells are completed to forfeit $100 $^{00}/_{100}$ for each well there after not completed as above set forth. It is understood that all the terms and conditions between the parties hereto shall extend and apply to their respective heirs executors administrators and assigns. In case the first well is not a paying well second party is to surrender this lease and the said $300 $^{00}/_{100}$ deposited is to revert to second party. In Witness Whereof the said parties have hereinto set their hands and seals the day and year first above written.

In Presence of	G. H. HARMAN	(*seal*)
W. C. CORDREY	W. H. WHITMAN	(*seal*)
STEPHEN A. AUGUS	Wm L. CONNELLY	(*seal*)

State Ohio
County of Wood } ss

On this 21st day of February A.D. 1895 before me a Notary Public in and for said County personally appeared the above named G. H. Harman and W. H. Whitman and acknowledged that they did sign and seal the within instrument and the same is their free act and deed for the use and purposes therein named.

(*notarial*)   STEPHEN A. AUGUS

(*seal*)   *Notary Public*

In consideration of the sum of Two Hundred Dollars to me in hand paid by Charles B. Johnson and Herman Phillips of Toledo Ohio I do hereby transfer to said parties two thirds interest in the within lease subject to the terms thereof. Dated at Toledo, O March 29 1895

Witnesses.   W. L. CONNELLY   (*seal*)

Received April 3rd 1895   CHRIS FINKBEINES
Recorded April 10th 1895   *Recorder*

This lease was written in longhand, for in 1895 there were no standard lease forms.—W.L.C.

INDEX

This book has been printed direct from type and is set in Linotype Old Style No. 7. It is a type which has outstanding legibility, a soothing evenness of color on the page, and compact fitting of the individual letters. While it lacks some of the *character* of many other book faces in general use, it is sound and comfortable. It does its job in a straightforward manner, without any frills or eccentricities, and thus seemed an appropriate type choice for this similarly straightforward book.

UNIVERSITY OF OKLAHOMA PRESS : NORMAN